Hawaiian Prayers for Life Events

by
Kahu Wendell Kalanikapuaenui Silva

Book Design & Illustrations
Ruth Moen

Published by
Hawai'i Cultural Services (HCS) P. O. Box 4782, Kāne'ohe Hawai'i

HAWAIIAN PRAYERS FOR LIFE EVENTS

ISBN – 978-0-9860122-3-5

First Printing: August, 2020
Printed in Hawaiʻi, USA

Book Design and Illustrations: Ruth Moon, Dog & Pony Show

Contact the Publisher:
Wendell P. K. Silva
Hawaiʻi Cultural Services
P. O. Box 4782
Kāneʻohe, Hawaiʻi 96744
www.kahunateachings.com

Distributed by:
Hawaiʻi Cultural Services
info@HawaiiCulturalServices.com

This book entitled: *Hawaiian Prayers for Life Events* celebrates the 20th anniversary of Kahu Wendell Kalanikapuaenui Silva's spiritual ministry in Hawaiʻi. A portion of the proceeds from the sale of this book will be used to support the furtherance of educational, cultural and spiritual enrichment programs offered by the Ke Aloha o Kalani Ministry. The contents of this book are intended exclusively for informational, cultural and educational purposes only and not for personal choices or decisions.

KA HOʻOLAʻA ʻANA
Dedication

No kuʻu wahine, koʻu kōkoʻolua ʻO Kalona a me ka ʻohana o māua, kēia puke.
This book is dedicated to my loving wife and lifelong partner, Sharon and our family.

ME KA HOʻOMAIKAʻI
Acknowledgements

Mahalo nui loa iā ʻoukou āpau no kā ʻoukou kōkua me kēia puke.

My heartfelt gratitude to the following individuals who directly or indirectly assisted with production, design and publication of this book.

No kuʻu mau kūpuna, kuʻu mau kumu aʻo.
To my venerable ancestors, my teachers.

No Kauaholopali Silva, kuʻu kumu alakaʻi.
To Kauaholopali Silva, cultural resource.

No Kinitia Derosier, ka hoa kūkākūka.
To Cynthia Derosier, publishing consultant.

No Luka Moen, ke kanaka kaha kiʻi a hoʻolele huakēpau.
To Ruth Moen, cover design, illustrations, production and typesetting.

No Konala Carreira Ching, ka luna hoʻoponopono.
To Donald Carreira Ching, editor.

No Linika Voellmy, ka lima ʻākau.
To Linda Voellmy, volunteer.

No Kahu Alalani Hill, ka mea kākoʻo.
To Reverend Alalani Hill, supporter.

No kuʻu ʻohana nui a me nā makamaka āpau.
To my extended family and many friends.

No nā haku o nā puke Hawaiʻi.
To the authors of Hawaiian Books.

KA PAPA KUHIKUHI
The Table of Contents

KA PAPA KUHIKUHI
The Table of Contents

KA ʻŌLELO AʻO
Linguistic Note

The Hawaiian language in this book has been presented in a simplified traditional and non-academic form. Instead of providing a glossary of terms, the Hawaiian words used in the introductory narratives and prayers are presented in bold face type and their English translation equivalents are printed in plain text in parentheses.

Additionally, in accordance with the recommendation of my **kūpuna** (elder) mentors, I have chosen to use the **ʻokina** (glottal stop) and the **kahakō** (macron) to help with the pronunciation of the Hawaiian words. For those who may not be familiar with the Hawaiian language, it may be helpful to use a Hawaiian-English Dictionary with diacritical marks as a personal guide and reference.

Finally, Hawaiian is a beautiful language. Many words have several meanings as well as different levels of translation and interpretation. Some translations reflect the figurative or spiritual rather than literal expression of the language. The Hawaiian terms used in this text and their definitions are not meant to be authoritative or absolute.

Ola no ka mea Akua, make no ka mea Akua ʻole.
He who has a God lives; He who has no God dies.

Pukui, Mary Kawena. ʻŌlelo Noʻeau. # 2492

This proverb expresses the heart and soul of traditional Hawaiian spirituality. It describes the profound faith and intimate personal relationship that the early Hawaiians subjectively shared with their **Akua** *(God).*

KA MANA'O MUA
Foreword

Hawaiian Prayers for Life Events is a unique, one-of-a-kind resource book of Hawaiian pule. Inspired by the past and reflective of the present, this collection offers a treasure trove of traditional and contemporary prayers that spiritually commemorate life's most precious moments, memorable occasions and meaningful experiences. Through pule we call **ke akua,** as well as our **aumakua, kini akua** and **kupuna** for guidance and assistance.

With the exception of the **Kumulipo** (Hawaiian creation chant), **Pule Ho'omaika'i I Ka Mea 'ai** (Mealtime Grace) and the **Ka Pule A Ka Haku** (Lord's Prayer), all of the pule were created by Kahu Kalanikapuaenui Silva. Kahu Silva is a **Kanaka 'Ōiwi** faith leader, currently celebrating his twentieth year of ministerial services in Hawai'i. Kahu was raised in a **kanaka 'ohana** tied to generational ancestral ways, and has been mindful and respectful of early Hawaiian spiritual practices, ceremonial liturgy and prayer traditions.

Each **pule** is presented in **'ōlelo makuahine** with English translations to ensure that the **mana,** cultural authenticity and spiritual integrity are preserved and perpetuated. Composed for private as well as communal use, many of the **pule** in this book reflect similar spiritual beliefs, value systems and teachings that early Hawaiians shared in common with a variety of other faiths.

While many people today have differing religious philosophies and beliefs, most people share similar needs and intents around prayers as a form of worship. Whatever your spiritual path in life, it is hoped that the **pule** included in this anthology will inspire you to ask, receive and give your blessings for a wide variety of personal intentions, special needs and life events. We are beyond fortunate that Kahu Silva is sharing his invaluable **mana'o** as a **kupuna, kahu, kumu** and **haku puke** in this deeply needed *Hawaiian Prayers for Life Events*—**e pule kakou!**

with gratitude and aloha,

Maile Meyer,
Founder, Nā Mea Hawai'i/Native Books

KA ʻŌLELO MUA
Introduction

Ka poʻe kahiko (The ancient Hawaiians) were a deeply spiritual people. They embraced the belief that the universe originated from a mysterious energy source that is manifested in all of creation. Contrary to many other religions, the early Hawaiians considered all **Akua** (Gods) deserving of respect and worship. They viewed their **Akua** (deities) as awe inspiring, omnipotent spirit beings who were to be both feared and revered.

Living in spiritual oneness with the terrestrial realm of nature, the indigenous Hawaiians actively venerated as many as four hundred thousand major and lesser gods and goddesses. The major **Akua** (gods) and more prominent deities were formally enshrined and worshipped in consecrated temple structures called **heiau** or in **wahi kapu** (sacred sites). The multitude of lesser deities whose names were too numerous to mention were hallowed collectively and traditionally acknowledged in prayer offerings as **nā kini akua** (the divine pantheon).

Similar to the gods of Greek mythology, the Hawaiian **Akua** (deities) not only possessed supernatural qualities, they also embodied many human characteristics and were able to assume a wide variety of **kino lau** (earthly forms). Some of these spirit beings actually lived on the earth and interacted spiritually and terrestrially with humans. Others resided in mythical places whose origins have remained hidden since time immemorial in the corners of remote antiquity.

In the days of old Hawaiʻi, **pule** (prayer) was an integral part of the daily lifestyle of the Hawaiian people. The early Hawaiians loved to pray. They offered an infinite variety of prayers for almost every occasion, event, activity, and special need. Pule provided the primary means for them to establish a personal relationship and communicate with the gods. While the manner, method, purpose, and nature of the pule may have differed, prayer was the most expeditious way for a person to spiritually cultivate the favor of the Gods and acquire **mana** (spiritual power).

Mana can be best described as a non-physical form of energy originating from the **Akua** (Gods) that is innate in the nature of all existence. There are two types of mana: that which is inherent and that which could be acquired. The ancient Hawaiians firmly believed that the act of pule was a potent source for the sending and/or receiving of mana. Mana could also be transmitted from one source to another ritually or gained through the learning and developing of a specialized skill, talent, knowledge and ability. According to Hawaiian tradition, legendary heroes and ordinary people were able to accomplish amazing feats, superhuman deeds and perform miracles by means of the mana acquired through the power of pule.

It is said that the melodic sound and poetic imagery of the Hawaiian language offered in a prayer styling was especially pleasing to the Akua. Therefore, the offering of a pule also required choosing the most beautiful words in the Hawaiian language which best communicated a person's meaningful intentions. However, it is also believed that the **aloha** (devotion) of the supplicant and the manner in which the pule is delivered is also very important to ensuring the power of a prayer.

In the traditional Hawaiian society, **kāhuna pule** (priests) were trained as masters of prayer and ceremonial ritual. They were known to possess such great mana that they were able to pray an animal or person to death, to heal the sick, and even restore life. Prayers of the **kāhuna** (priestly) and **ali'i** (chiefly) classes were often very formal, subject to taboo restrictions and traditionally required stringent spiritual protocol. These prayers were more often performed with strict liturgical rites and sacred rituals. On the other hand, prayers performed by the **maka'āinana** (common folk) tended to be more spontaneous, less formal and usually recited in a conversational style to ask blessings **mai ka na'au** (from the heart). With the exception of those pule restricted by priestly or chiefly **kapu** (taboo), prayers could be offered by anyone at any time, any place, and for any reason.

To access the more powerful Akua, some Hawaiians would invoke the assistance of their **'aumākua** (ancestral guardian spirits) to serve as spiritual intercessors for the family in times of need. Similar to the celestial beings which other cultures

spiritually refer to as guardian angels, the ʻAumākua were considered an essential part of everyday family life in the islands. Although not as powerful as the major **akua** (deities), they were fervently revered and respected as spiritual sentinels and protectors for the family. Traditionally, ʻaumākua images were customarily accorded a place of honor in the home, placed on a **kuahu** (altar) and worshipped in prayer with other effigies.

With the fall of the ancient religion at the hands of the chiefs in 1819 and the arrival of the missionaries in 1820, the old religion of the kahuna and the pagan ways of the native Hawaiian gave way to the wave of Christianity. Christianity proliferated and quickly became the predominate religion of the 19th century Hawaiian people. During this period, many of the traditional prayers shared between the early Hawaiians and their ancient gods began to change and adapt to the ever-changing times. However, whether Christian or not, many Hawaiians today still continue to offer ancient pule and incorporate traditional ceremonial protocols as the occasion may warrant.

Hawaiian Prayers for Life Events is not intended as an academic treatise on Hawaiian language, religion, or spirituality. It represents a heartfelt effort and a personal contribution toward encouraging the furtherance of the Hawaiian language, culture and prayer traditions as a precious legacy **mai nā kūpuna mai** (from the cherished Hawaiian ancestors).

ADDITIONAL PUBLICATIONS

By Kahu Silva

Hawaiian Birth Signs—Nā Hō'ailona Hānau—The Hawaiian Lunar Calendar. [Audiobook CD], 2012.

Hawaiian Birth Signs—Nā Hō'ailona Hānau—The Hawaiian Lunar Calendar, 2013.

'Ano Lani; 'Ano Honua, A Spiritual Guide to the Hawaiian Lunar Calendar, 2017.

'Ano Lani; 'Ano Honua Hawaiian Mystic Moon Chart 2019-2020. [Chart], 2018.

Silva, Wendell P.K., (Editor.). (1984), Nānā i Nā Loea Hula, Kalihi-Palama Culture & Arts Society, Inc.

E PILI ANA I KE KANAKA KĀKAU

About the Author

Kahu Wendell P. Kalanikapuaenui Silva is a highly renowned Native Hawaiian faith leader, **kahuna pule** (prayer expert), **kumu a'o** (teacher), **kanaka 'i'imi 'ike** (scholar), **loea** (cultural resource) and **mea kākau** (author). He descends from a prominent ancestral lineage of Hawaiian spiritual healers and shamanistic practitioners that have kept their sacred teachings secret for centuries. Internationally recognized for his expertise in Hawaiian prayer offerings, blessing rites, ceremonial rituals and spiritual protocols, he remains one of the very few chosen keepers of Hawai'i's traditional spiritual arts. Kahu Silva has dedicated much of his lifetime toward preserving and perpetuating the legacy of ancient wisdom and knowledge entrusted to him by his esteemed Hawaiian ancestors and the cherished cultural luminaries of his time.

He currently serves as **Kahu Nui** (Senior Pastor) of the **Ke Aloha O Kalani Ministry** (non-profit 501c3), a non-denominational church and fellowship that celebrates Hawaiian cultural values and values within Hawai'i's unique multi-ethnic society.

A highly respected cultural leader proclaimed a "living treasure" by the City & County of Honolulu, he has the distinction of being appointed the first Native Hawaiian Executive Director of the Hawai'i State Foundation on Culture and the Arts. Kahu continues to spiritually and culturally serve the Hawai'i community through the offering of a variety of learning opportunities on Hawaiian holistic spiritual healing and traditional divination techniques. He is extensively involved with numerous culture and arts programs and projects in Hawai'i.

E Pule Kākou

Let Us Pray

NĀ AKUA
The Heavenly Ones

KUMULIPO – The Hawaiian Creation Chant

Hā ke akua i ka lewalani, ka hā o kona waha.
From the breath of the Creator came forth the cosmos.

THE AGE OF DARKNESS

One of the earliest traditional Hawaiian accounts linking the world of the living to the realm of the gods is a cosmological prayer chant called the **Kumulipo** (Song of Creation). Revered as one of the most sacred mantras of the Native Hawaiian people, it shares a similarity to the biblical version of the origins of the universe as recorded in the text of Genesis. This ancient **mele** (Hawaiian prayer chant) articulates in detail the creation of the firmament, the formation of the earth, and the emergence of **kānaka** (humans).

PROLOGUE TO THE "AGE OF DARKNESS"

In the beginning, the earth was hot.
At that time, the heavens unfolded and formed the sky.
The first light of dawn began to appear.
The moon illuminated the heavens.

Makali'i (the Pleiades) appeared in the night.
From the substance of the earth, land was established.
From the source of the darkness came forth the darkness.
From the depths of the darkness came the night.
The darkness seemed endless
The darkness obscured the sun;
The darkness of the night
It is the night
The night gave birth
Kumulipo was born of the night, a male
Pō'ele was born of the night, a female

English Translation by:
Kahu Kalanikapuaenui Silva

KUMULIPO

‘O ke au i kāhuli wela ka honua
‘O ke au i kāhuli lole ka lani
‘O ke au i kūka‘iaka ka lā
Ho‘omālamalama i ka malama
‘O ke au ‘O Makali‘i i ka pō
‘O ka walewale ho‘okumu honua ia
‘O ke kumu o ka lipo i lipo ai
‘O ke kumu o ka pō i pō ai

‘O ka lipolipo, ‘O ka lipolipo
‘O ka lipo o ka lā
‘O ka lipo o ka pō
Pō wale ho‘i
Hānau ka pō
Hānau Kumulipo i ka pō, he kāne
Hānau Pō‘ele i ka pō, he wahine

Text from Beckwith, Martha, W/.ed/,
The Kumulipo: A Hawaiian Creation Chant
Chicago: University of Chicago Press, 1951; pg.42

PULE 'AUMĀKUA – Ancestral Deities Prayer

He hikuhiku nā kiniakua.
The host of the gods are many, many.

Pukui, Mary Kawena. 'Ōlelo No'eau. # 577.

NĀ 'AUMĀKUA – Ancestral Guardians

Among the pantheon of deities, worshiped by the ancient Hawaiians were the **'aumākua** (ancestral spirits). Similar to guardian angels, they served as spiritual advisors, intercessors, messengers and protectors of individuals and their family. The early Hawaiians traditionally embraced the 'aumākua deities as revered members of their **'ohana** (family) and venerated their presence with honorific prayer offerings and ceremonial rituals. This pule may be used to contact and/or to re-establish a relationship with one's family 'aumākua.

THE ANCESTRAL DEITIES PRAYER

O my Ancestral Guardians of antiquity,
The Spiritual Sentinels of the light,
The Heavenly Beings above,
The Divine Ones of the earth below,
I call upon all of You now.
Behold Your descendant
______________________(name).
If it pleases all of You
Arise and reveal
Your great supernatural powers.
Be watchful and continue to protect me from
harmful shades of the night.
Guard against the evil doers of darkness.
Shield me
From the malintents and the causes of trouble.
Guide my life's journey
On the path of righteousness.
Grant me blessings of Your mana.
The prayer has been offered.
All is free.

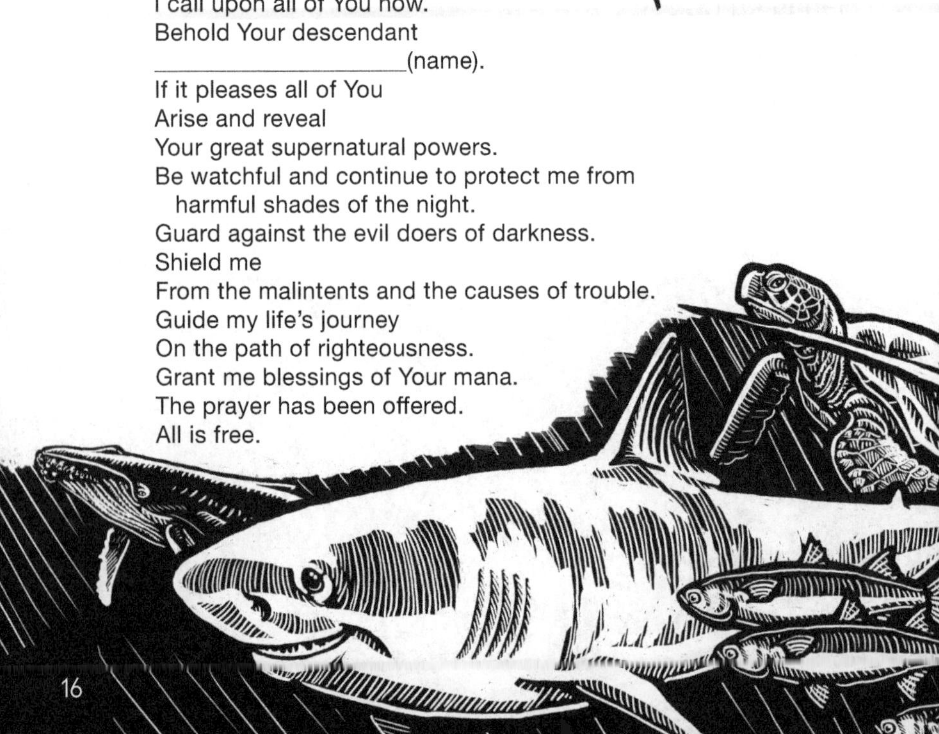

PULE ʻAUMĀKUA

E oʻu mau ʻAumākua mai ka pō mai,
E oʻu mau ʻAumākua mai ke ao,
Ka paʻa iluna,
Ka paʻa ilalo,
Ke hea aku nei au iā ʻOukou.
Eia kā ʻOukou pulapula
ʻO____________________(inoa).
E ʻoluʻolu ʻOukou,
E ala mai a e hōʻike mai nei
I kō ʻOukou mana nui.
E nānā a e mālama ʻOukou iaʻu
  mai ka ʻUhane ʻino o ka pō ʻē.
E kiaʻi aku i nā hana ʻino o ka pō ʻē.
E pale aku ʻOukou
Mai nā manaʻo ʻino a me
Nā hoʻopilikia ʻana iaʻu.
E alakaʻi mai ʻOukou iaʻu
Ma ke ala maikaʻi.
E hō mai i ka mana.
ʻĀmama. Ua noa.

PULE HO`ONANI – Adoration Prayer

'Ike 'ia ke alo kapu o Ke Akua i ka nani o ke ao.
The presence of the Divine is revealed in the beauty of nature.

HO'ONANI – Adoration

Living on a remote archipelago of tiny islands in the middle of the vast Pacific Ocean, the indigenous Hawaiians relied on the resources of their environs to sustain them and they developed a rich culture that was deeply rooted in the **'āina** (land), **ke kai** (the sea) and **ka lani** (sky). They held the belief that the spirit essence of their **akua** (deities) is manifest in all of existence. Composed in the traditional Hawaiian style, the poetic lyrics of this Pule Ho'onani metaphorically glorify the divine presence of the akua as it is revealed in nature and beheld in the wonders of all of creation.

ADORATION PRAYER

With every sunrise
And sunset,
I behold Your sacred presence,
In the beauty of all creation,
In the moonlight and the twinkling stars,
In the billowing cloud banks,
In the heavenly blessings of the rain,
In the arching of the multi-hued rainbow,
In majestic mountains lofty grandeur,
In the verdure of the upland forest,
In the variety of tropical blooms,
In the sway of the palm fronds,
In the gentle touch of a pleasant breeze.
I hear the sound of Your voice,
In the melody of sweet birdsongs,
In the whispering of the sea,
In the waves of the ocean.
This prayer is affectionately offered to
  You, O Divine Akua from the depths of my soul.
The prayer is ended.
All is free.

PULE HO'ONANI

Mai ka pi'ina a ka lā,
A ka welona a ka lā,
Ke 'ike aku nei wau ma Kou alo,
I ka nani o ke ao holo'oko'a,
I ka mahina a me nā hōkū,
I nā pae 'opua,
I ka ua kahiko o ka lani,
I ka pipi'o 'ana mai o ke ānuenue,
I nā mauna ki'eki'e,
I ka uluwehi o ka uka,
I nā pua like 'ole o ka 'āina,
I ka lau o ka niu ani pe'ahi,
I ka pā makani ahe 'olu'olu.
Ke lohe aku nei au i Kou leo,
I ke kani o nā manu,
I ke kai hāwanawana,
I nā nalu o ka moana.
He kānaenae aloha ka'u nou,
E Ke Akua mai ka na'au.
'Āmama. Ua noa.

KA PULE A KA HAKU – The Lord's Prayer

No ka mea, Nou ke aupuni, a me ka mana a me ka hoʻonani ʻia, a mau loa aku.
For thine is the kingdom, the power and the glory, forever and ever.

THE OUR FATHER

With the arrival of missionaries in 1820, came the dawn of Christianity. Christian teachings and prayers were subsequently introduced to Hawaiʻi. These poignant words were reverently spoken by the Lord Jesus over 2,000 years ago when he taught his disciples how to pray. It is recorded in the scripture of the New Testament of the Bible according to Matthew 6:9 -13 and Luke 11:2 - 4. Known in Hawaiian as **Ka Pule A Ka Haku** (The Lord's Prayer), it continues to be recited as one of the most honorific and spiritually powerful Christian prayers of all time.

THE LORD'S PRAYER

Our Father who art in heaven,
Hallowed be Thy name,
Thy kingdom come;
Thy will be done
On earth as it is in Heaven.
Give us this day
Our daily bread;
Forgive us our trespasses,
As we forgive those
Who trespass against us
And lead us not into temptation;
but deliver us from evil;
For Thine is the kingdom, the power and the glory, forever and ever.

—Amen

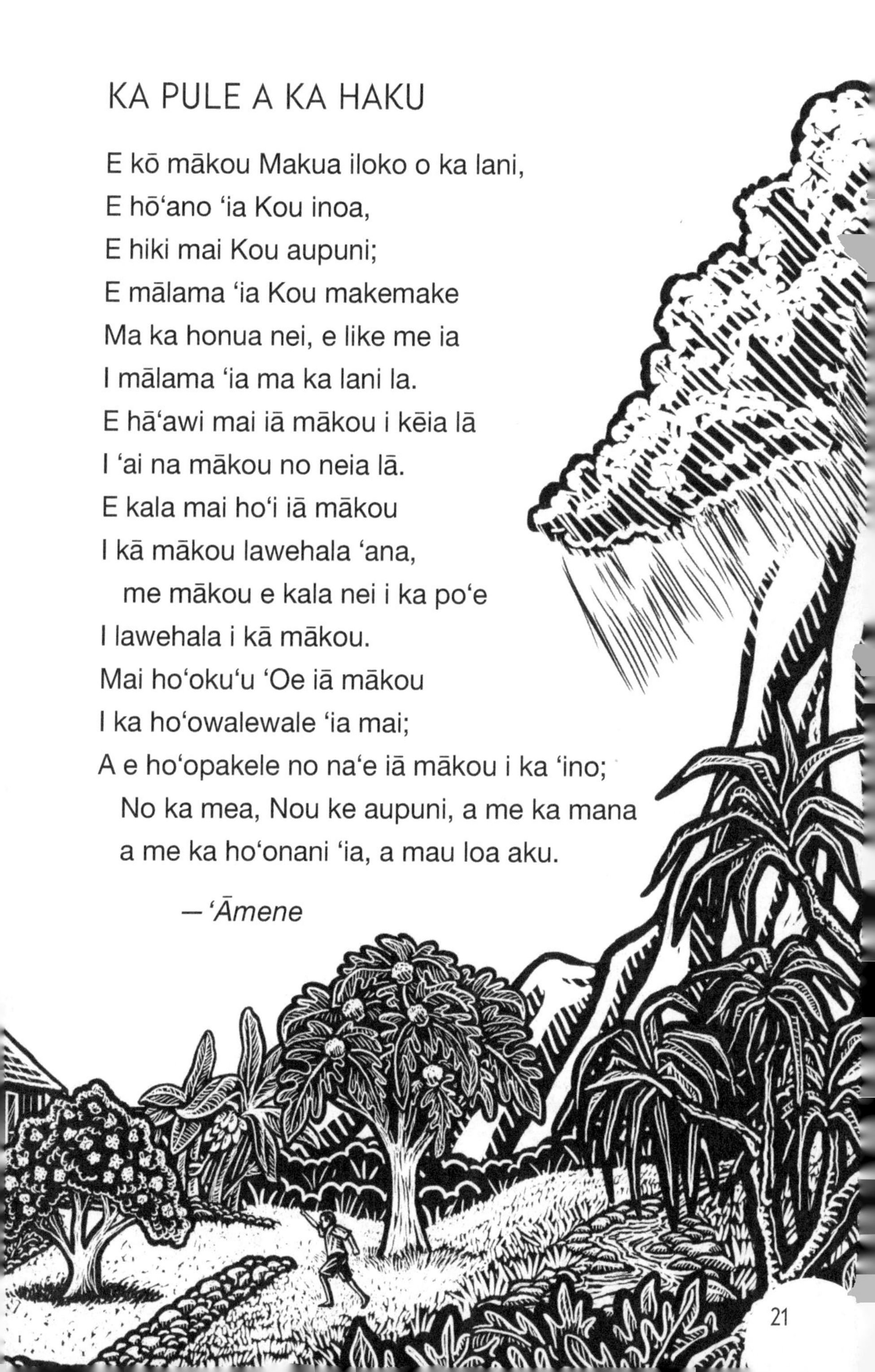

KA PULE A KA HAKU

E kō mākou Makua iloko o ka lani,
E hō'ano 'ia Kou inoa,
E hiki mai Kou aupuni;
E mālama 'ia Kou makemake
Ma ka honua nei, e like me ia
I mālama 'ia ma ka lani la.
E hā'awi mai iā mākou i kēia lā
I 'ai na mākou no neia lā.
E kala mai ho'i iā mākou
I kā mākou lawehala 'ana,
me mākou e kala nei i ka po'e
I lawehala i kā mākou.
Mai ho'oku'u 'Oe iā mākou
I ka ho'owalewale 'ia mai;
A e ho'opakele no na'e iā mākou i ka 'ino;
No ka mea, Nou ke aupuni, a me ka mana
a me ka ho'onani 'ia, a mau loa aku.

— *'Āmene*

NĀ PULE NO KA LĀ
Prayers for the Day

PULE NO KA LĀ – Morning Prayer

Ao ka pō, ā pō ke ao.
Night becomes day, until day becomes night.

KE AO – The Dawn

The early Hawaiians spiritually associated the energy of the rising sun with the God Kū, whom they also venerated as the patriarch of the Hawaiian family. They considered the dawn of each and every day as a heavenly blessing and traditionally greeted **wana'ao** (the dawn's early light) with the offering of a morning prayer asking for a good and productive day. This Pule No Ka Lā celebrates the precious gift of life and seeks to obtain the spiritual guidance necessary to successfully overcome the obstacles, challenges and misfortunes that the new day may bring.

PRAYER FOR THE DAY

I dedicate this day to You,
O sacred Akua,
The One who reigns supreme over the realms of
the heavens and the earth.
Here is Your humble servant,
______________________(name).
On this special day, I fervently pledge
my heartfelt devotion to You,
In thought, words and deeds.
Guide me with Thy divine wisdom.

Fill my being with Thy righteousness.
Shield me now
From the causes of afflictions.
Empower my spirit with Thy **mana** (supernatural power).

Here is the prayer offering that I humbly
share in Thy sacred presence.

—Amen

PULE NO KA LĀ

Ke hoʻolaʻa nei au i neia lā iā ʻOe,
E Ke Akua,
Ka Mea nana i hana i ka lani a me ka honua.
Eia Kāu kauwā,
ʻO______________________(inoa).
I kēia lā, ke hoʻohiki nei au i kuʻu aloha iā ʻOe,
Ma ka noʻonoʻo ʻana, nā ʻōlelo ʻoluʻolu, a me nā hana pono.
E alakaʻi mai ʻOe iaʻu me Kou akamai.
E hoʻopiha mai ʻOe iaʻu ma Kou pono.
E hoʻopale aku nei iaʻu
Mai nā hoʻopilikia ʻana.
E hoʻoikaika mai ʻOe iaʻu me Kou mana nui.
Eia ka pule a Kāu kauwā nei e haipule ai i mua o Kou alo.

—*ʻĀmene*

PULE AWAKEA – Midday Prayer

Kau ka lā i ka lolo, ho'i ke aka i ke kino.
When the noonday sun is overhead, the earthly shadow retreats into the body.

Pukui, Mary Kawena. 'Ōlelo No'eau. #1611.

AWAKEA – High Noon

High noon begins when the sun crosses a location's meridian and reaches the zenith or its highest point in the heavens. It is the time of day when the solar energy of the sun is at its maximum. Associated with **Wākea** who is revered as the mythical ancestor of all Hawaiians, awakea is traditionally considered a very auspicious time for performing prayer offerings, ceremonial rituals and spiritual healing rites. This pule is used to unite the body, mind and spirit in oneness with the realm of the cosmos and to harness the **mana** (life giving energy) of the sun.

MIDDAY PRAYER

O Celestial Source of heavenly light,
From the rising of the sun,
To the setting of the sun,
Behold Thy servant,
________________(name).
I beseech You now.
Tis the zenith of Your glory.
Reveal the splendor of Thy radiant solar light.
Strengthen my spirit essence
With Thy divine cosmic energy.
Illuminate my thoughts with Thy sacred wisdom.
Bestow health and wellness.
It is within Thy power to grant, O God.
All is free.

PULE AWAKEA

E Ke Kumu o ke ao lani,
Mai ka puka ʻana o ka lā,
A ke komohana a ka lā,
Eia Kāu kauwā,
ʻO ______________(inoa).
Ke noi aku nei au iā ʻOe.
ʻO ke awakea nei.
Hō'ike aʻe ʻOe i Kou nani.
E hōʻikaika mai ʻOe i koʻu ʻuhane
Me Kou mana nui.
E hoʻomālamalama mai ʻOe
I kuʻu manaʻo me Kou manaʻo akamai.
E hō mai i ke ola pono.
ʻO Kāu ia, e ke Akua, e hāʻawi ai.
ʻĀmama.

PULE AHIAHI – Evening Prayer

Ke hoʻolaʻa nei mākou i kēia pō mahina iā ʻOukou, e Nā Akua o ka lewalani.
We dedicate this lunar night to you, the celestial deities of the heavens.

AHIAHI – Evening

The early Hawaiians were governed by a synodic lunar calendar. In ancient times, the initial sighting of the moon at **ahiahi** (sunset) not only traditionally ushered in **ka pō** (the nightly realm of the gods), it also officially marked the beginning of a new day in the Hawaiian Islands. Pule Ahiahi is customarily performed during **ka napoʻo ʻana o ka lā** (the setting of the sun). Composed in the traditional Hawaiian style, it is used to greet the heavenly shades of nightfall, welcome the new day, and summon forth the family ancestral **akua** and **ʻaumākua** (deities) to bestow divine blessings on their earthly descendants.

HAWAIIAN EVENING PRAYER

At the setting of the sun
To the point when evening draws to a close
There comes the dark corner of the night.

Night reigns in the realm of the heavens
And reaches this earthly place.
Blessings abound
From the night.

Kāne, God of light,
Eternal and supreme
It is You who blesses
The stars in the vast heaven.

Lono, God of the calm night,
It is indeed perfect clarity
That continues to be released
For all of us.

Hina, the celestial Goddess
Who dwells in the moon.
Reveal Your radiant beauty
In the divine light of wisdom.

Ye ancestral Guardians of remote antiquity.
Here are Your descendants.
It is we who go forth in the night
With our great affection for You.

We call upon all of You now
To grant good health,
Knowledge and spiritual power
For each of us.

Here is our prayer
Given with humility
The prayer is finished.
All is free.

PULE AHIAHI

I ka welona o ka lā
A pili i ke ahiahi
Aia hoʻi ke kihi
O ka pō.

Kū ka pō ma ka lani
Ma kēia honua nei.
E hoʻomaikaʻi
Ka pō.

E Kāne o ke ao,
Pauʻole a holoʻokoʻa
Nāu e hoʻomaikaʻi ana
I nā hōkū ma ka lani
ākea.

E Lono i ka pō laʻi laʻi,
O ke ʻalaneo nō hoʻi
E kuʻua mai ana
No mākou ā pau.

E Hina, ke Akua wahine
E noho ana ma ka
mahina,
E hōʻike mai ʻOe
i Kou nani
I ka mālamalama.

E nā ʻAumākua o ka pō,
Eia kā ʻOukou mau
kawowo.
Na mākou e hele ana
i ka pō.

Ke hea aku nei mākou
iā ʻOukou
E hō mai ʻOukou i ke ola
Me ka ʻike a me
ka mana
No mākou pākahi.

Eia kā mākou mau
pule kāhea
E hāʻawi ʻia aku nei me
ka haʻahaʻa.
ʻĀmama. Ua noa.

PULE ʻOHANA – Family Prayer Gathering

O ka makua ke koʻo o ka hale e paʻa ai.
The parent is the support that holds the household together.

Pukui, Mary Kawena. ʻŌlelo Noʻeau. #2424.

ʻOHANA – Family

ʻOhana is the Hawaiian word for family, relative, kin, group and clan. It describes the continuing generations of offspring that descend from a kupuna or common ancestral progenitor. The term ʻohana also means to gather for family prayers. Traditionally, many Hawaiian families designated a time to unite their ʻohana spiritually in prayer, to socially strengthen kinship ties and acknowledge their family's cosmological relationship to their heavenly deities. The following may be used for such family prayer gatherings.

FAMILY PRAYER

We dedicate this day to You,
O divine Akua.
Here is our family,
United in the Hawaiian spirit of aloha.
We are gathered together now
To share our family prayer offering.
We are only human and finite in our earthly nature,
We ask Your forgiveness of our limitations.
We beseech You now to bestow Your blessings.
Shield us from the causes of misfortune.
Guide us with Your divine wisdom.
Give all of us good health.
Grant the ability to see things clearly,
And empower each of us with Your Holy Spirit.
Please favorably receive our fervent prayer offering.

—Amen

PULE ʻOHANA

Ke hoʻolaʻa nei mākou i kēia lā iā ʻOe,
E ke Akua.
Eia nei kō mākou ʻohana,
Hui pū ʻia me ke aloha.
Ke hoʻākoakoa mai nei mākou
No ka pule ʻohana.
He poʻe hewa mākou,
E huikala mai nei ʻOe.
Ke noi aku nei mākou i Kou pōmaikaʻi.
E hoʻopale aku iā mākou
Mai nā hoʻopilikia ʻana.
E alakaʻi mai iā mākou me Kou akamai.
E hāʻawi mai i ke ola no mākou āpau.
E hō mai i ka ʻike pono a me ka mana
No mākou pākahi.
E lohe ʻOe me ka ʻolu i kā mākou pule aku.

—ʻĀmene

KA LĀ HIKI Ā KA LĀ KAU
The Life Cycle

PULE HO'OLA'A I KE KEIKI – Baby Blessing Prayer

He lei poina 'ole ke keiki.
A lei never forgotten is the beloved child.

Pukui, Mary Kawena. 'Ōlelo No'eau. # 740.

KA HO'OLA'A 'ANA – The Dedication

In ancient Hawai'i, the birth of a **keiki** (child), especially the **hiapo** (first born) was considered one of the greatest blessings bestowed upon the family by the heavenly Akua. Hawaiians customarily celebrated this precious gift of life with prayer offerings, sacred ceremonial rituals and feasting. Adapted from a traditional Hawaiian prayer, the following **pule ho'ola'a 'ana** (dedicatory prayer) may be used to consecrate a baby on the occasion of his or her birth and as an invocation at a child's **'aha 'aina piha makahiki** (first birthday lū'au feast).

BABY BLESSING

O Divine Source of everlasting love,
Here is a child born of the land,
______________________(name)
A beloved boy/girl child.
Take good care of him/her
Until he/she seeks a career vocation.
Bestow on him/her Thy divine grace
And the heavenly virtues of faith, hope and compassion.
Grant knowledge of things great and small.
Guide him/her on the upright path.
Fill his/her life with much happiness,
And a lifetime of many good years
To obtain life's precious blessings.
It is within Thy power to grant, O Ke Akua.
Let the taboo be lifted.
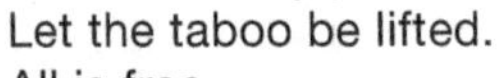
All is free.

PULE HOʻOLAʻA I KE KEIKI

E ke Akua, Ke Kumu o ke aloha mau,
Eia ke keiki hānau ʻia o ka ʻāina,
ʻO__________________ (inoa)
He keiki kāne/kaikamahine.
E mālama iāia ā nui aʻe
A ʻimi i kāna ʻoihana.
E hoʻomaikaʻi iāia
Me ka manaʻo iʻo, ka manaʻo lana,
A me ke aloha i nā mea āpau.
E hō aku i ka ʻike nui a me ka ʻike iki.
E alakaʻi iāia ma ke ala kūpono.
E hoʻopiha i kona ola me ka hauʻoli loa
A me nā makahiki maikaʻi a piha nui
A loaʻa ke ola pōmaikaʻi.
ʻO Kāu ia, e ke Akua,
e hāʻawi ai.
ʻĀmama. Ua noa.

PULE NO KA LĀ HĀNAU – Birthday Blessing

'O ka lā nui, ka lā hānau.
Happy birthday wishes.

KA LĀ HĀNAU – The Birthday

In Hawai'i, a person's **lā hānau** (birthday) is considered a very important rite of passage. Each year marks a milestone that an individual has successfully achieved on the journey of life. Such an auspicious occasion is customarily celebrated in the islands with a gathering of family and friends at a **pā'ina** (dinner party) or **'aha'aina** (large banquet). The following prayer may be performed as an invocation for such an event. It asks special blessings for the birthday celebrant, gives thanks for the nourishing food that has been prepared and honors the presence of all the guests attending the event.

BIRTHDAY BLESSINGS

O Divine Akua,
The Source of the heavens and the earth,
Here are our family and our dear friends united together
in the spirit of aloha.
We are gathered on this joyous occasion to celebrate
the birthday of____________________(name).
We beseech You now,
To bless him/her with health, happiness and prosperity.
Bless the food that has been prepared to nourish us
and our honored guests.
Grant long life for all of us.
Please accept this humble prayer
Offered in the name of love and peace.

—*Amen*

PULE NO KA LĀ HĀNAU

E ke Akua,
Ke Kumu o ka lani a me ka honua,
Eia kō mākou ʻohana, a me kō mākou mau
hoaloha, e hui pūʻia me ke aloha.
Ke hoʻākoakoa ʻia nei mākou,
I kēia hanana piha me ka hauʻoli,
No ka hoʻolauleʻa ʻana i ka lā hānau
ʻO_______________________(inoa).
Ke noi aku nei mākou iā ʻOe,
E hoʻomaikaʻi aku iāia me ke ola,
Me ka hauʻoli loa a me Kou pōmaikaʻi.
E hoʻomaikaʻi i nā mea ʻai nei, i hoʻomākaukau ʻia
na mākou, a me nā mea i kono ʻia.
E hō mai i ke ola loa no mākou āpau.
E ʻoluʻolu ʻOe, loaʻa kēia haipule,
Hāʻawi ʻia me ke aloha a me ka maluhia.

— *ʻĀmene*

PULE HOʻĀO – Marriage Prayer

Awaiāulu Ke Aloha.
Love made fast by tying together.

Pukui, Mary Kawena. ʻŌlelo Noʻeau. # 245.

HOʻĀO – Marriage

Hoʻāo is the old Hawaiian term for marriage. It literally translates "to stay until daylight." Hoʻāo also refers to the night of the day called Huna, the eleventh night of the lunar month when traditional Hawaiian wedding nuptials took place. Inspired by an ancient chant, this marriage prayer spiritually celebrates the qualities of **aloha** (true love) as the greatest of all treasures and acknowledges it as the eternal foundation upon which is built a happy marriage and an enduring home. This Pule Hoʻāo befittingly concludes asking blessings upon the couple and extending best wishes for a beautiful new life as husband and wife.

MARRIAGE PRAYER

Love has made a plea to unite you both
As one in body, mind, and spirit
For a lifetime.
You both are now securely bound
In the everlasting garland of marriage,
From season to season unending.
Cherish always
This blessing of true love
With hearts affectionately joined.
For genuine love is
The greatest of life's treasures.
It is a very precious gift that comes from Our Heavenly Creator.
May the divine Akua bless you both forever in a beautiful life.
The prayer is offered.
All is free.

PULE HO'ĀO

Na ke aloha i kono iā 'olua e hui pū
Ma ke kino, ma ka mana'o,
A me ka 'uhane,
No ke ola pili mau.
Ke awaiāulu 'ia nei 'olua
I ka lei male'ana
No nā kau ā kau.
E hi'ipoi mau ana 'olua
I kēia aloha maoli
Me ka lōkahi o ka pu'uwai.
No ka mea,
He mea waiwai loa, ke aloha.
He makana makamae ia
Mai kō mākou Makualani mai.
Na ke Akua e ho'omaika'i iā 'olua
Me ke ola pono. 'Āmama. Ua Noa.

PULE KAU I KA HANO – Honorific Prayer

ʻIke ʻia nō ka loea i kāna ʻano hana.
An expert is recognized by the quality of his/her workmanship.

KAU I KA HANO – Confering Honor

In Hawaiʻi today, when a person achieves distinction, it is customary to recognize the honoree and celebrate the occasion with the ceremonial presentation of a **palapala hoʻokō** (certificate of achievement), **hoʻokupu** (tribute) or **makana** (gift). This prayer acknowledges the successful personal accomplishments of an individual that continue to serve as a source of pride and an inspiration for others. It may be offered as an invocation for an awards presentation ceremony, promotion, military change of command or a graduation party.

HONORIFIC PRAYER

O Holy Spirit,
The Source of divine wisdom,
We are gathered together
On this joyous occasion
To honor
_______________(name)
Who has strived for the highest
And has reached the pinnacle of success
In his/her many endeavors.
We beseech You now
To bless him/her
With Your continuing care,
Your protection, and great love.
Guide his/her future life's directions.
Grant him/her the gifts of good health and much happiness.
It is indeed within Your power, O God,
To bestow these things.

—Amen

PULE KAU I KA HANO

E Ka ʻUhane Hemolele,
Ke Kumu o ka naʻauao,
Ke hoʻākoakoa ʻia nei mākou
I kēia hanana piha me ka hauʻoli
No ka hoʻohiwahiwa ʻana
Iā ______________(inoa)
Ka mea i kūlia i ka nuʻu
A kū i ka niʻo
Ma kāna mau hana.
Ke noi aku nei mākou iā ʻOe
E hoʻomaikaʻi iāia
Me Kāu mālama mau ʻana,
Kou malu, a me Kou aloha nui.
E alakaʻi iāia mai kēia wā aku.
E hō aku iāia i ke ola maikaʻi a me ka hauʻoli nui.
Nāu nō ia, e ke Akua,
E hāʻawi ai.

— *ʻĀmene*

PULE HO'OMAHA LOA – Retirement Prayer

Pau ka hana! He manawa kēia no ka ho'omaha loa 'ana.
The work is finished! This is a time for retiring.

HO'OMAHA LOA – Retirement

Retirement marks the beginnning of a new stage of life for people. Retirees now have the freedom and privilege to choose how to spend their time. In Hawai'i, when a person retires from a job, it is customary to celebrate the occasion festively with a **pā'ina** (party) or banquet feast called **'aha 'aina**. This Pule Ho'omaha Loa is appropriate and suitable for use as an invocation at retirement ceremonies. It asks special blessings for the retiree and acknowledges the successful career accomplishments of the individual.

RETIREMENT PRAYER

O Almighty God,
We come forth now
With heads bowed in reverence
Before Thy divine presence.
We are gathered together
On this joyous occasion
To celebrate the retirement of
____________________(name)
Who has strived for the highest
In his/her career endeavors.
We beseech You now
To bless him/her
With Your continuing care,
Your protection and Your benevolence.
Grant him/her blessings of good health and much happiness.
It is indeed within Your power, O God,
To grant these things.

—Amen

PULE HOʻOMAHA LOA

E ke Akua mana loa,
Ke hele mai nei mākou
Me kō mākou mau poʻo kūlou
I mua o Kou alo kapu.
Ke hoʻākoakoa ʻia nei mākou
I kēia hanana piha me ka hauʻoli
No ka hoʻomaha loa ʻana
ʻO ______________(inoa)
Ka mea i kūlia i ka nuʻu
Ma kāna mau ʻoihana āpau.
Ke noi aku nei mākou iā ʻOe
E hoʻomaikaʻi iāia
Me Kāu mālama mau,
Kou malu, a me Kou aloha nui.
E hō aku iāia i ke ola maikaʻi
A me ka hauʻoli nui.
Nāu nō ia, e ke Akua,
E hāʻawi aku.

— *ʻĀmene*

PULE MĀLAMA MAU – Hospice Prayer

I kanaka no ʻoe ke mālama i ke kanaka.
You will be well served when you care for the person who cares for you.

Pukui, Mary Kawena. ʻŌlelo Noʻeau. # 1185.

MĀLAMA MAU – Continuing Care

Hospice care in old Hawaiʻi was customarily embraced as an inherent **ʻohana** (family) tradition. Spiritually associated with the Hawaiian deity, Kāne, the Creator and giver of life, caring for a terminally ill **kupuna** (elder) or relative was naturally expected and considered as a genuine labor of love. This Pule Mālama Mau is meant to help a person to spiritually prepare for the transition of the essence of their ethereal life force from the physical world of the living to the ancestral spiritual realm of the unseen.

HOSPICE PRAYER

O Akua, the Divine Source of all life,
During this time of my illness,
Please help me to overcome
The dread of the words that I must hear,
The fear of choices that I must make,
The pain that I must endure and suffer,
The deeds that I must do or let be done
In the coming days ahead.
Before I lay myself to rest in sleep,
I choose now to forgive others and
Ask to be forgiven.
Remove any bitterness in my heart
And fill my being with love forever.
Please hear my prayer!

—Amen

PULE MĀLAMA MAU

E ke Akua, ke Kumu hoʻokahi o ke ola āpau,
ʻOiai i kēia manawa o koʻu ʻōmaʻimaʻi,
E kōkua ʻOe iaʻu e hoʻopio mai
I ka weli o nā huaʻōlelo aʻu e lohe ai,
I ka makaʻu o nā koho aʻu e hoʻoholo ai,
I ka ʻeha aʻu e kāmau a e ʻīnea ai,
I nā mea aʻu e hana ai a e hanaʻia ai
I nā lā e hele mai nei.
Ma mua o koʻu moe ʻana e hoʻomaha loa,
E koho wau e kala i nā kānaka ʻē aʻe
A e noi e kala ʻia mai ana.
E hoʻopau i ka hulialana ma koʻu naʻau
A e hoʻopiha iaʻu me ke aloha mau.
E lohe ʻOe me ka ʻolu i kaʻu pule aku.

—*ʻĀmene*

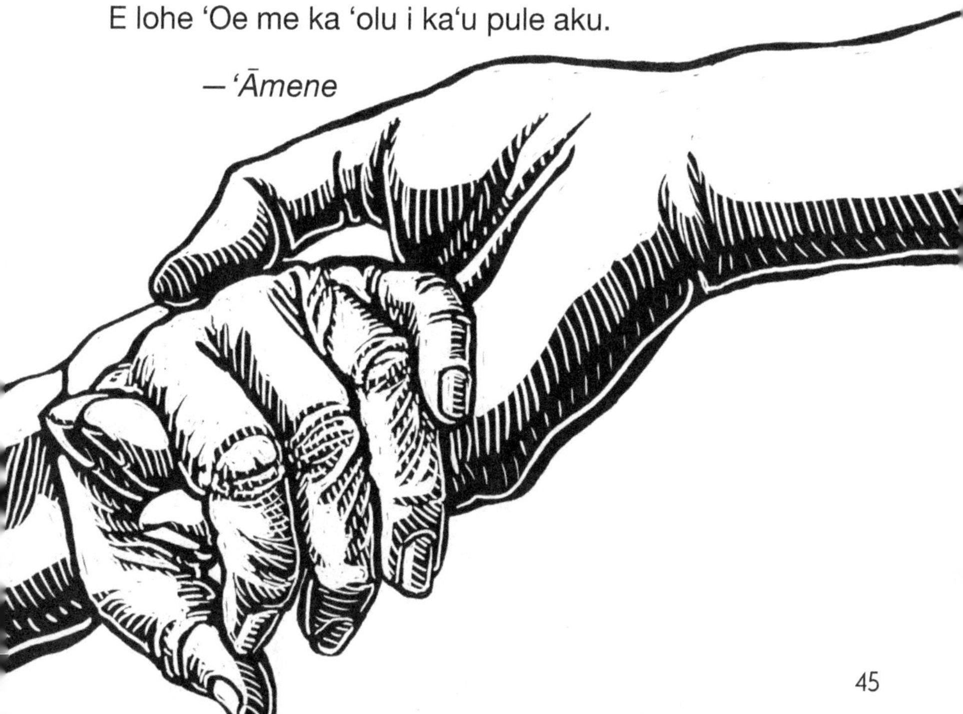

PULE HO'OMANA'O – Memorial Prayer

Ua hala 'oia i ke ala ho'i'ole mai.
He/she has gone on the road from which there is no return.

Pukui, Mary Kawena. 'Ōlelo No'eau. # 420.

HO'OMANA'O – Remembrance

According to Hawaiian tradition, it is said that in death the **'uhane** (soul) leaves the body and is thought to hover on earth near the deceased's remains for several days after a person's passing and until it is guided into the realm of **pō** (the domain of the gods). This **Pule Ho'omana'o** (memorial prayer) combines our traditional Ke Aloha o Kalani Ministry teachings with ancient Hawaiian spiritual beliefs. It calls upon the family's **'aumākua** (angelic guardian spirits) to welcome and guide the soul of the dearly departed loved one into the realm of eternal bliss and the kingdom of paradise.

MEMORIAL PRAYER

O Almighty God,
Who sets before us,
the ways of life and death.
Ye Guardian Spirits of remote antiquity,
Ye ancestral Angelic Beings of the light,
I now summon forth all of You.
Here is your beloved descendant,
______________________________(name).
A good man/woman who has departed this earthly life.
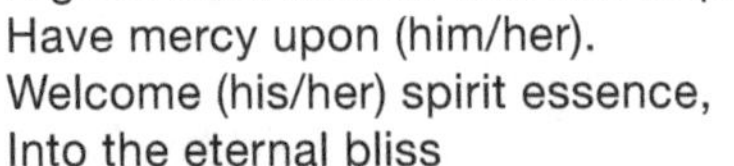
Have mercy upon (him/her).
Welcome (his/her) spirit essence,
Into the eternal bliss
Of Your heavenly kingdom.
Grant unto (him/her) peace and rest
From season to season unending.

—Amen

PULE HOʻOMANAʻO

E ke Akua mana loa,
E hoʻomākaukau ai i ke alahele o mākou,
O nā mea o ke ola a me ka make.
E nā ʻAumakua mai ka pō mai,
E nā ʻAumakua o ke ao,
Ke hea aku nei au iā ʻOukou āpau.
Eia mai kā ʻOukou pulapula i hala aku
ʻO__________________ (inoa).
He kāne/wahine maikaʻi i hele loa.
E aloha aku iāia.
E hoʻokipa a'e i kona ʻuhane
Iloko o ka ʻoliʻoli mau
O Kou aupunilani.
E hoʻomalu mai nei iāia
No nā kau ā kau.

— *ʻĀmene*

NĀ PULE PONOʻĪ
Personal Prayers

PULE HO'OMANA – Prayer for Empowerment

'Ike no i ka lā o ka 'ike; mana no i ka lā o ka mana.
Know in the day of knowing; mana in the day of mana.

Pukui, Mary Kawena. 'Ōlelo No'eau. # 1212.

HO'OMANA – Spiritual Empowerment

The Hawaiian term **ho'omana** means to empower spiritually. Derived from the root word **mana** (spiritual power), it literally refers to the conveying of a miraculous form of non-physical energy that originates from a divine source and exists in all of nature. Traditionally, early Hawaiians believed that their deities possessed large reservoirs of mana that could be spiritually accessed and/or acquired by humans through prayer offerings, religious rites and ceremonial rituals. This Pule Ho'omana seeks the imparting of mana for the purpose of synergistically unifying the body, mind and spirit.

PRAYER FOR EMPOWERMENT

Greetings of aloha to You,
O almighty **Akua** (God).
Behold Your devoted servant,
_______________________(name).
I graciously ask Your benevolence.
Sanctify me with Thy blessings.
Empower my spirit essence
With Thy divine cosmic energy.
Strengthen my physical self.
Help me to spiritually overcome the forces of evil,
jealousy and causes of misfortune.
Bestow upon me continued wellness.
Here is my fervent prayer offering,
Given in the name of love and peace.
The prayer is said. The taboo is lifted.

PULE HOʻOMANA

ʻAnoʻai me ke aloha,
E Ke Akua mana loa.
Eia Kāu kauwā,
ʻO _____________(inoa).
Ke noi aku nei au i Kou ʻoluʻolu.
E hoʻomaikaʻi mai ʻOe iaʻu.
E hoʻomana mai ʻOe i koʻu ʻuhane
Me Kou mana nui.
E hōʻikaika mai i koʻu ola kino.
E kōkua mai iaʻu e hoʻopio i ka
Manaʻo ino, ka lili a me nā hoʻopōpilikia ʻana.
E hō mai i ke ola mau.
Eia kaʻu haipule e hāʻawi ʻia nei,
Ma ka inoa o ke aloha a me ka maluhia. ʻĀmama.

PULE PALE – Prayer for Protection

He ko‘e ka pule a kahuna, he moe no a ‘oni mai.
The prayer of a kahuna is like a worm; it may lie dorment but it will wiggle along.

Pukui, Mary Kawena. ‘Ōlelo No‘eau. # 699.

‘ANĀ‘ANĀ – Sorcery

The early Hawaiians acknowledged the power of sorcery and the influence that practitioners of the art of black magic had on their daily lifestyle. They held the belief that certain ailments, mental illnesses, loss of physical body functions and even death were caused by **hana ‘ino** (evil sorcery) performed by **kāhuna ‘anā‘anā** (master sorcerers). This Pule Pale beckons the benevolent family deities to protect and shield the supplicant from sources of spiritual harm and malevolence. It is used to ward off the forces of evil and to help spiritually prevent the suffering of any potential misfortune.

PRAYER FOR PROTECTION

O Omnipotent Spirit of God,
Come forth.
I implore You,
Be vigilant, be protective,
Shield me from malintent, jealousy and malevolence of any kind.
Ward off the causes of troubles and the evil deeds of
my adversaries.
Shelter me now beneath Thy protective spiritual mantle.
Strengthen my spirit with Thy divine power.
Let not the shadow of fear intimidate me.
(For) You are my heavenly sanctuary.
I place now my well-being in Your good hands.
Profound is the kapu; profound is its freeing.

PULE PALE

E Ke Akua Mana Loa,
Maʻaneʻi mai.
Ke noi aku nei au iā ʻOe,
E hoʻokiaʻi, e hoʻomālama,
E hoʻopale aku nei iaʻu
Mai ka manaʻo ino, ka lili a me nā hoʻopilikia ʻana.
E pale aku nei i nā pōpilikia,
a me nā hana ʻino a nā ʻenemi.
E hoʻomalu mai ʻOe iaʻu malalo o Kou ʻaʻahu kaua.
E hoʻoikaika mai ʻOe i koʻu ʻuhane me Kou
mana nui.
ʻAʻole makaʻu au i nā mea e weli ai.
ʻO ʻOe ka puʻuhonua nani noʻu.
Ke waiho nei au i koʻu ola i Kou mau lima maikaʻi.
ʻEliʻeli kapu; ʻeliʻeli noa.

PULE HO'OMĀLAMALAMA – Prayer for Enlightenment

Nou, kēia lamakū o ka na'auao.
For you, this torch of wisdom.

HO'OMĀLAMALAMA – Enlightenment

Ho'omālamalama literally means "to illuminate or enlighten." It describes a state of mind that empowers an individual to perceive and experience the living cosmos as it is beheld in the light of life. Inspired by faith and reason, it spiritually represents the acquisition of knowledge that enables a person to better understand the world and improve their own living conditions. The early Hawaiians strongly encouraged the seeking of **na'auao** (wisdom) as an important traditional value. This Pule Ho'omālamalama is an appeal for blessings of divine guidance, spiritual enlightenment and the power of discerning what is spiritually **pono** (right) and **hewa** (wrong).

PRAYER FOR ENLIGHTENMENT

O Holy Spirit,
The Guiding Light of knowledge,
I beseech Thee now
To shine forth the light of Thy countenance upon this humble servant.
Enlighten my thoughts with the gift of Thy undeniable truth.
For, truth is unchangeable.
Grant me the ability to clearly see the important things in life.
Fill my heart with Thy never-ending aloha.
Strengthen my spirit with Thy all powerful divine energy.
Be with me always, O Ke Akua.
Here is my prayer.

—Amen

PULE HOʻOMĀLAMALAMA

E Ka ʻUhane Hemolele,
ʻO ʻOe Ke Kukui o ka mālamalama,
Ke noi aku nei au iā ʻOe
E kau mai i Kou mālamalama maluna
o Kāu kauwā.
E hoʻomālamalama i koʻu mau manaʻo me ka ʻike
o Kou ʻoiaʻiʻo.
No ka mea, he ʻonipaʻa ka ʻoiaʻiʻo.
E hō mai i ka ʻike e ʻike nui.
E hoʻopiha ʻOe i koʻu naʻau me Kou aloha mau.
E hoʻoikaika i koʻu ʻuhane me Kou mana nui.
Eia ke Akua me aʻu i nā wā āpau
Eia kaʻu haipule.

—ʻĀmene

PULE KŌKUA – Prayer for Help

Kōkua aku, kōkua mai.
Help others, be helped.

KŌKUA – Help

Kōkua is the Hawaiian word for help, aid, support and assistance. Like so many people throughout the world, in times of difficulty and distress, the early Hawaiians turned to supernatural beings they called Akua to hear their lament and answer their personal prayer plea for help. The nature of these prayers for assistance were usually spontaneous and heartfelt. The following Pule Kōkua was inspired by Psalm 102: 1, 2 from the Bible's treasured collection of venerable hymnal verses. It extends an earnest appeal for spiritual help in overcoming the **pilikia** (trials and tribulations) that life sometimes brings.

PRAYER FOR HELP

Hearken unto me,
O Ever Merciful God,
And let my cry come unto Thee.
Do not turn away from me
In this my hour of desperation.
For You, Ke Akua, are my Guardian,
My Refuge, my Strength.
I trust in You implicitly.
Therefore, I beseech You
Please help me to successfully overcome
My life's current trials and tribulations.
Heed my fervent prayer offering.
Answer my spiritual plea for assistance.
I place now my well-being in Your good hands.

—Amen

PULE KŌKUA

‘Auhea wale ana ‘Oe,
E ke Akua o ke aloha mau,
A e ho‘okomo aku i
Ka‘u kāhea ‘ana i mua Ou.
Mai hūnā ‘Oe i Kou maka mai ā a‘u mai
I kēia hola o‘u e nele ai.
‘O ‘Oe, e Ke Akua, ku‘u Kia‘i,
  ku‘u Pu‘uhonua, a me ku‘u Ikaika.
Hilina‘i wau iā ‘Oe.
E ‘olu‘olu ‘Oe,
E kōkua mai ‘Oe ia‘u e ho‘opio
I nā pōpilikia o kēia manawa.
E lohe ‘Oe me ka ‘olu i ka‘u pule aku.
E kōkua mai ia‘u.
Ke waiho nei au i ko‘u ola i Kou
  mau lima maika‘i.

—‘Āmene

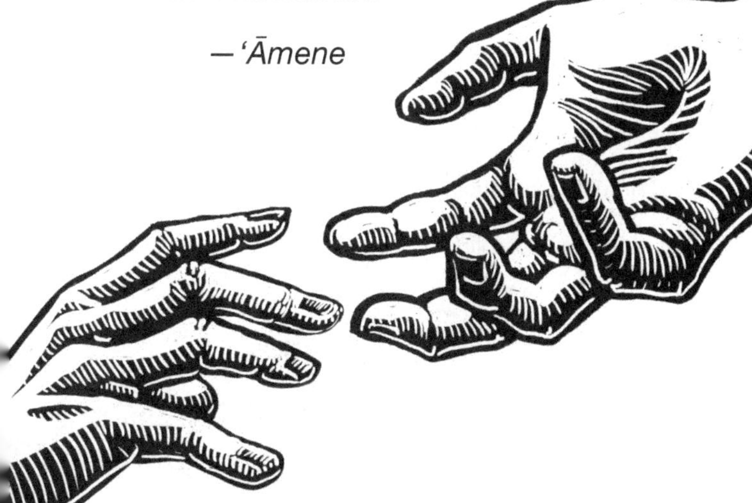

PULE KŪIKAWĀ – Provisional Prayer

Pule no ka mea pono.
Prayer for a special intention.

KŪIKAWĀ – Standing in Time

Similar to the Roman Catholic novena, this Pule Kūikawā seeks the granting of a special intention or personal request. It is a provisional prayer that is normally performed while standing or kneeling before a representative icon and recited for nine consecutive days or weeks. If the specific prayer request is granted prior to or at the end of the petition period, customarily, the supplicant is traditionally expected to reciprocate with a **ho'okupu** (tribute), spiritual gift offering or perform a charitable deed of kindness for others as an expression of gratitude for the benevolence and favor received.

PROVISIONAL PRAYER

Look upon me with Thy favor,
O Heavenly Akua.
Heed this special plea of Thy servant,
____________________(name).
I beseech Thee now.
Have mercy on me,
In this hour of my desperation.
Please, I implore You,
Help me now
To overcome my troubles.
Lift now the yoke
Of my weary burdens.
Strengthen my spirit essence
With Your divine energy.
Bestow health and well-being.
Grant my special intention.
You are my Spiritual Foundation, You are my Guardian,
You are my Refuge.
In You, I place now my complete trust.

—Amen

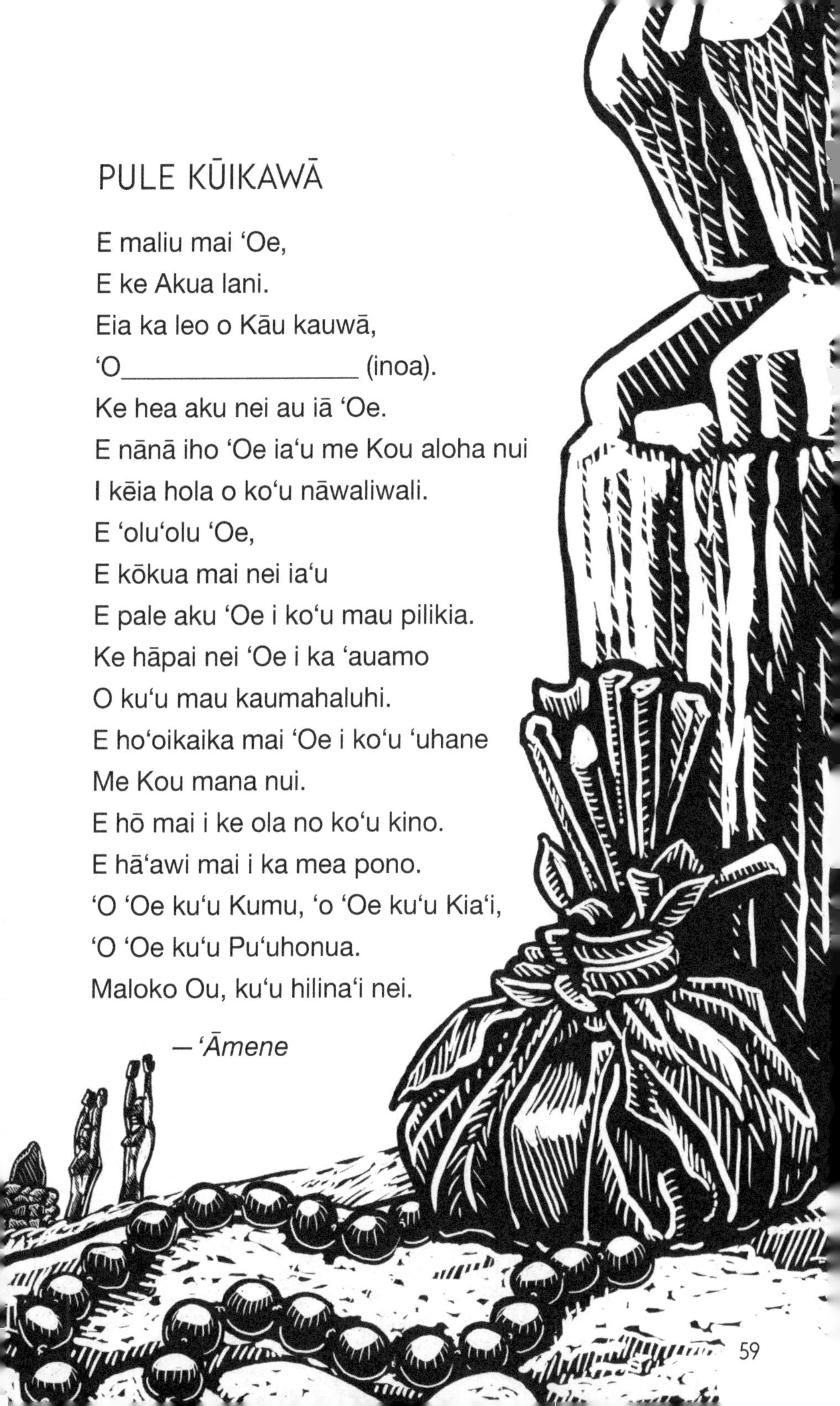

PULE KŪIKAWĀ

E maliu mai ʻOe,
E ke Akua lani.
Eia ka leo o Kāu kauwā,
ʻO_________________ (inoa).
Ke hea aku nei au iā ʻOe.
E nānā iho ʻOe iaʻu me Kou aloha nui
I kēia hola o koʻu nāwaliwali.
E ʻoluʻolu ʻOe,
E kōkua mai nei iaʻu
E pale aku ʻOe i koʻu mau pilikia.
Ke hāpai nei ʻOe i ka ʻauamo
O kuʻu mau kaumahaluhi.
E hoʻoikaika mai ʻOe i koʻu ʻuhane
Me Kou mana nui.
E hō mai i ke ola no koʻu kino.
E hāʻawi mai i ka mea pono.
ʻO ʻOe kuʻu Kumu, ʻo ʻOe kuʻu Kiaʻi,
ʻO ʻOe kuʻu Puʻuhonua.
Maloko Ou, kuʻu hilinaʻi nei.

—ʻĀmene

PULE MALUHIA – Prayer for Inner Peace

ʻAʻohe pueo keʻu, ʻaʻohe ʻalae kani,
ʻaʻohe ʻūlili holoholo kahakai.
No owl hoots, no mudhen cries, no ʻūlili runs on the beach.
There is perfect peace.

Pukui, Mary Kawena. ʻŌlelo Noʻeau. # 207.

MALUHIA – Serenity

Derived from the root word **malu** (peace) and the passive imperative suffix **hia**, the term maluhia translates as a state of tranquility. Spiritually, it describes the awe and solemnity that reigned during some of Hawaiʻi's ancient taboo ceremonies. This Pule Maluhia is intended for those who are searching for a moment of solace and "peace of mind" during a time of stress, turmoil or uncertainty in their lives. Similar to a prayer for serenity, it is used to help an individual resolve personal enigmas, circumvent obstacles and successfully overcome the numerous challenges that are frequently encountered in today's modern high-tech world.

PRAYER FOR INNER PEACE

O Holy Spirit,
Free my thoughts
From life's everyday cares and woes.
Give me the courage
To successfully overcome life's challenges
And the wisdom
To make the right choices.
Bless me now with peace of mind.

—Amen

PULE MALUHIA

E ka ʻUhane Hemolele,
E hoʻokaʻawale ʻOe i koʻu mau manaʻo
Mai nā pōpilikia nui a me nā hopohopo.
E hāʻawi mai iaʻu i ka wiwoʻole
E holopapa i nā mea e hiki ana iaʻu
A me ka naʻauao e hoʻoholo
I nā koho pololei.
E hō mai nei iaʻu i ka maluhia.

—ʻĀmene

PULE HUIKALA – Prayer for Forgiveness

ʻAʻohe mea make i ka hewa; make no i mihi ʻole.
No one has ever died for the mistakes he has made;
only because he didn't repent.

Pukui, Mary Kawena. ʻŌlelo Noʻeau. # 188.

HUIKALA – Forgiveness

Huikala is a Hawaiian word that means to absolve, free completely, pardon entirely and forgive all iniquities. It also describes a traditional spiritual cleansing and purification ritual ceremonially performed by **kāhuna** (priests) to release a person from any physical, spiritual and emotional faults. Similar to the Catholic sacrament of Confession, huikala requires that the offender confess, repent, and make restitution. This Pule Huikala is used as a Hawaiian act of contrition to spiritually free a person from prior transgressions and to absolve a penitent of any and all wrong-doings or sins committed.

PRAYER FOR FORGIVENESS

O merciful God,
The divine Source of all existence,
I am truly sorry for my various transgressions.
I offer my heartfelt repentance for the wrongs that
  I have committed in thought, word and deed.
I beseech now Thy mercy.
Grant me forgiveness.
Absolve me of my past iniquities.
Deliver me from every evil.
Grant me Your redeeming grace.
Cleanse now my soul.
The prayer is finished. The taboo is lifted.

PULE HUIKALA

E ke Akua o ke aloha mau,
Ke Kumu o nā mea āpau,
Hilahila loa iho au
No ka nui o ka'u mau lawehala.
Ke mihi aku nei au i ka'u mau hewa,
Ma ka mana'o, ma ka 'ōlelo, a ma ka hana.
Ke noi aku nei au i Kou aloha.
E kala mai ia'u.
E ho'oku'u 'Oe i ka'u mau hewa i ka wā mamua.
E ho'opakele mai 'Oe ia'u i nā mea 'ino.
E ho'omaika'i mai 'Oe ia'u.
E ho'oma'ema'e mai i ku'u 'uhane.
'Āmama. Ua Noa.

PULE HOʻOMAIKAʻI – Personal Blessing

I luna nā maka, ilalo nā kuli. E pule kākou.
Eyes up, knees down. Let us pray.

Pukui, Mary Kawena. ʻŌlelo Noʻeau. # 1230.

HOʻOMAIKAʻI – Blessings

Since time immemorial, people have lifted their voices in prayer petitions to their respective deities in order to cultivate their favor and to receive their benevolence in return. It remains one of the most common type of spiritual expressions used to acknowledge and honor the existence of God. The early Hawaiians loved to pray. They prayed for almost anything and everything in life. This Pule Hoʻomaikaʻi traditionally seeks blessings of spiritual guidance, divine wisdom and good health for the supplicant. It is also appropriate for recitation as a **pule no ka lā** (prayer for the day) or as a particular occasion may warrant.

PERSONAL BLESSING PRAYER

O heavenly Akua (God),
I offer You now my heartfelt devotion.
I beseech Thee now,
Bestow upon me the benevolent virtues
Of faith, hope, and love.
Enlighten my thoughts with the light of Thy divine wisdom.
Sanctify my spirit essence.
Guide me on the path of righteousness.
Grant me health and well-being.
This prayer is fervently offered to You,
O all merciful Akua,
With my never-ending adoration.

—*Amen*

PULE HOʻOMAIKAʻI

E ke Akua,
Ke aloha aku nei au iā ʻOe
Me koʻu naʻau.
Ke hea aku nei au iā ʻOe,
E hāʻawi mai ʻOe iaʻu i ke kalakia
O ka manaʻoʻiʻo, o ka manaʻolana,
A me ke aloha.
E hoʻomālamalama mai ʻOe iaʻu
Me Kou manaʻo akamai.
E hoʻohemolele mai i koʻu ʻuhane.
E kaʻi iho iaʻu ma ke ala maikaʻi.
E hō mai i ke ola.
He kānaenae aloha kaʻu Nou,
E ke Akua lokomaikaʻi,
Me kuʻu aloha pauʻole.

— *ʻĀmene*

PULE HOʻŌLA – Healing Prayer

He waiwai nui ke olakino maikaʻi.
Good health is precious.

HOʻŌLA HOU – Restoring Health

The ancient Hawaiian **kāhuna lāʻau lapaʻau** (herbal healers) strongly believed in the power of prayer. Prior to initiating their therapeutic herbal treatment, they customarily offered prayers to spiritually facilitate the patient's medical healing process. This **Pule Hoʻōla** (Healing Prayer) was composed for an individual afflicted with the COVID-19 Corona virus and may be used to help restore the health and spiritual well-being for those who have other types of illnesses.

HEALING PRAYER

O Heavenly God,
I ask your divine grace.
Lovingly embrace Thy servant,
_________________________(name),
With Thy merciful heart.
Bestow Thy blessings upon him/her
Take away the pain, the throbbing, the ache
and all of the suffering
associated with his/her illness.
Comfort him/her in this time of distress.
Heal him/her of this ailment
Until the residuals no longer remain.
It is indeed within thy power, O God,
To restore his/her health.
Here is my humble prayer request,
which is offered with heartfelt aloha.
—Amen

Composed by: Rev. Kalanikapuaenui Silva
March 28, 2020

PULE HOʻŌLA

E ke Akua o ka lani,
Ke noi aku nei au i Kou pōmaikaʻi.
E aloha aku i Kāu kauwā,
Iā___________________(inoa)
Me Kou lokomaikaʻi.
E hoʻomaikaʻi iāia.
E lawe aku ʻOe i ka ʻeha, ke koni,
Ka huʻi a me nā ʻeha like ʻole āpau
O kona maʻi.
E hōʻoluʻolu aku ʻOe iāia.
E hoʻōla aku ʻOe iāia
A lawe aku i nā koena ā lilo loa.
Nāu nō ia, e ke Akua,
E hoʻōla aku iāia.
Eia ka haipule,
I hāʻawi ʻia me ka haʻahaʻa,
A me ke aloha.

— *ʻĀmene*

Haku ʻia e: Kahu Kalanikapuaenui Silva
March 28, 2020

PULE O KE KOA HAWAIʻI – A Soldier's Prayer

He hauʻoli ka ukali o ka lanakila.
Gladness follows in the wake of victory.

Pukui, Mary Kawena. ʻŌlelo Noʻeau. # 569.

PULE O KE KOA HAWAIʻI

I ka wā kahiko (In ancient times), when Hawaiian men and women went to war, they offered prayers asking for courage and seeking success in battle. It is said that the thoughts of their loved ones back home helped to inspire their bravery. This prayer was composed especially for Hawaiʻi's military service personnel preparing for a deployment overseas or prior to combat.

A SOLDIER'S PRAYER

O Holy Spirit,
Listen now to my call.
Behold Your servant,
_________________(name),
A soldier from Hawaiʻi.
I seek now and fervently
Ask Your blessings
And Your spiritual help.
Free me
From the shadow of fear
That pervades my thoughts.
Fill my being with Thy spiritual mana.
Hone my skills for combat.
Surround me now
With the shield of Thy divine battle armor.
Protect me now
From the harmful acts of warfare
And the enemies of our great nation.
Guide me now
On the pathway to victory.
I leave my life
In Your good hands.
Receive now this humble prayer
Offered with my never-ending devotion.
My prayer is ended. All is free.

PULE O KE KOA HAWAIʻI

E Ka ʻUhane o ke ao,
E hāliu mai nei ʻOe.
Eia Kāu kauwā,
ʻO_____________(inoa),
He koa mai Hawaiʻi.
Ke ʻimi a noi aku nei au
I Kou pōmaikaʻi
A me Kāu kōkua.
E hoʻokuʻu mai ʻOe iaʻu
Mai ka makaʻu o kuʻu manaʻo.
E hoʻopiha mai ʻOe iaʻu
Me Kou mana nui.
E hōʻoi iho iaʻu no ka paio.
E pōʻai mai iaʻu
Me ka pale kaua.
E pale mai ʻOe iaʻu
Mai nā hana ʻino
A nā enemi o ke aupuni.
E alakaʻi mai iaʻu
Ma ke ala o ka lanakila.
Ke waiho nei au i kuʻu ola
I Kou mau lima maikaʻi.
Eia ka haipule, i hāʻawi ʻia
Me koʻu aloha pauʻole.
ʻĀmama. Ua noa.

PULE NO NĀ HANANA
Special Occasion Prayers

PULE WEHENA – Opening Prayer

E waikāhi ka pono i mānalo.
It is well to be united in thought that all may have peace.

Pukui, Mary Kawena. ʻŌlelo Noʻeau. # 384.

KA HOʻOMAKA ʻANA – The Beginning

In Hawaiʻi, when a group of people gather together for the purpose of seeking spiritual guidance, sharing knowledge, and imparting wisdom, the ceremonial program of events customarily begins with an invocational prayer called a Pule Wehena. Traditionally performed by a **kahuna pule** (Hawaiian prayer expert), **kahu** (minister), **kupuna** (elder) or other spiritual designee, the following prayer invokes the presence of the Divine to spiritually bless the occasion and unite the participants holistically as **ʻohana** (family) in heart, mind and spirit. This prayer is considered appropriate for opening meetings, conferences, seminars, conventions, workshops, classes, lectures and various other types of group discussion sessions.

OPENING PRAYER

O Heavenly Akua,
The Spiritual Source of all existence,
We dedicate this day
And this special gathering to You.
We ask Your benevolent blessings
And seek now the light of knowledge.
Help us in our efforts to educate the unenlightened.
Fill each of us here with the essence of
  Your divine spiritual power.
Inspire the creativity that originates from the innermost
  depths of the soul.
Guide our thoughts in the spirit of wisdom.
Bestow upon us the gift of enlightenment.
It is within Your power to grant, O God.

—Amen

PULE WEHENA

E Ke Akua,
Ke Kumu o ke ao holo‘oko‘a,
Ke ho‘ola‘a nei mākou i kēia lā iā ‘Oe
A me kēia ‘aha kūkākūkā.
Ke noi aku nei mākou i Kou pōmaika‘i
A ke ‘imi aku nei mākou i ka na‘auao.
E kōkua mai ‘Oe iā mākou
E ho‘ona‘auao i nā kānaka na‘aupō.
E ho‘opiha ‘Oe iā mākou pākahi me
  Kou mana nui.
E ho‘oūlu iā mākou me ke a‘o loko
E ho‘okumu nei maloko o ka na‘au.
E alaka‘i i kō mākou mana‘o akamai.
E hō mai i ka ‘ike mālamalama.
‘O Kāu ia, e ke Akua, e hā‘awi ai.

— *‘Āmene*

PULE HO'OMAIKA'I I KA MEA 'AI – Mealtime Prayer

E ‘ai i ka mea i loa‘a.
What you have, eat.

Pukui, Mary Kawena. ‘Ōlelo No‘eau. # 251.

PULE HO'OMAIKA'I I KA MEA 'AI

Many of the early Hawaiian family customs and social relationships revolved around or involved food. Food was used as a means to unite the **‘ohana** (family) and friends, to celebrate special occasions and commemorate meaningful events. In ancient Hawai‘i, each food item not only had a nutritional relevence but also a spiritual significance. Customarily, before partaking of any food, a **pule** (prayer) was offered to spiritually give thanks to Ke Akua for the nourishing sustenance. Short and simple, this **Pule Ho‘omaika‘i I Ka Mea ‘ai** offering may be best shared as mealtime grace for informal family gatherings.

MEALTIME GRACE

God is great,
God is good,
Let us thank Him
For this food.
By His hands,
we all are fed.
Lord,
Give us now, our daily bread.

—Amen

Traditional Prayer

PULE HOʻOMAIKAʻI I KA MEA ʻAI

Nani Ke Akua,
Maikaʻi Ke Akua,
Ke hoʻomaikaʻi nei kākou lāia
Na kēia mea ʻai.
Ma Kona mau lima,
Ke hānai ʻia nei kākou āpau.
E ka Haku,
Ke hāʻawi mai nei iā mākou,
I ʻai na mākou o neia lā.

— ʻĀmene

Hawaiian Translation by
Kahu Kalanikapuaenui Silva

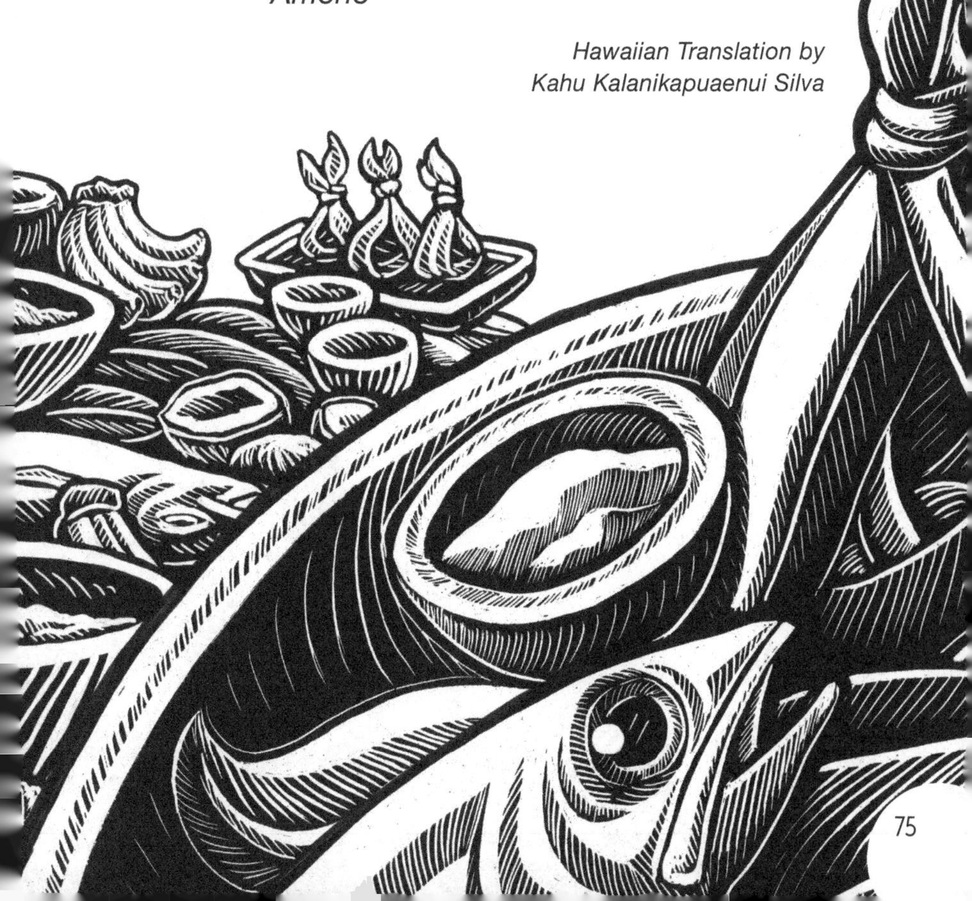

HOʻOMAIKAʻI I KA PAPA ʻAINA – Mealtime Prayer

ʻO ke aka ka ʻoukou, e ke Akua, ʻo ka ʻiʻo ka mākou.
Yours is the essence O God, ours the material part.

Pukui, Mary Kawena. ʻŌlelo Noʻeau. # 2448.

KA PAPA ʻAINA – The Meal

In ancient Hawaiʻi, each food item not only had a nutritional relevence but also a spiritual significance. Customarily, before partaking of any food, a calabash of **poi** (the Hawaiian staff of life) was uncovered and a **pule** (prayer) was offered to spiritually give thanks to Ke Akua for the nourishing sustenance. Under the old **kapu** (taboo) system, certain foods were prohibited to women who were also required to eat separately from the men. With the abolition of the **ʻai kapu** (eating taboo) by Hawaiʻi's Queen Kaʻahumanu in 1819, men and women were subsequently able to enjoy the freedom of sharing a meal together as a family.

MEALTIME PRAYER

O Heavenly Spirit of God,
Here are our family and friends
United together in the spirit of aloha.
We thank Thee, for this food, the fruits
of Thy bounty,
To nourish our body
And strengthen our souls.
Give us now ever grateful hearts
For this special day and this meal
That has been graciously prepared for us.
Help us to be ever mindful
Of the needs of others less fortunate.
Grant them Your heavenly protection.
We humbly now ask these blessings
of You.

—Amen

HO‘OMAIKA‘I I KA PAPA ‘AINA

E Ke Akua,
Eia kō mākou ‘ohana a me nā hoaloha
Hui pū ‘ia me ke aloha.
Mahalo ā nui loa,
Na kēia mau mea ‘ai,
I hānai ‘ia aku no kō mākou mau kino
A me ka ho‘oikaika ‘ana aku i
  kō mākou mau ‘uhane.
E hā‘awi mai iā mākou i ka na‘au ho‘omaika‘i ‘ia
No kēia lā a me kēia mau mea ‘ai
E ho‘omākaukau ‘ia na mākou.
E kōkua mai iā mākou
E ho‘omana‘o i nā po‘e ‘ilihune.
E hō aku iā lākou i Kou malu lani.
Ke noi aku nei mākou i kēia mau mea,
  me ka ha‘aha‘a.

—‘Āmene

HO'OMAIKA'I I KA HALE – House Blessing

O ka hale e kū, o ke kanaka e noho.
Where the house stands, there a person lives.

Pukui, Mary Kawena. 'Ōlelo No'eau. # 2402.

KA HALE – The House

In the days of old Hawai'i, a **hale** (house) was considered more than a structure used for protection, security and shelter from the elements. It served as the central gathering place for the **'ohana** (family) to celebrate their kinship, share their aloha and spiritually commune with their ancestral deities. The hale represented the heart and the soul of a family. It was the most important means of securing a family's physical and spiritual wellbeing. Traditionally, chiefs and commoners alike consecrated their homes prior to living in it. Inspired by an ancient Hawaiian prayer, this pule is used by Kahu for blessing a new or previously occupied home.

HOUSE BLESSING PRAYER

O Supreme God,
Ye Ancestral Guardians of antiquity,
Ye Divine Beings of the heavenly light,
Ye Spiritual Sentinels,
Behold Your devoted servant
______________________(name).
I beseech all of You now
To watch over this house
From above and below,
From corner to corner,
From sunrise until sunset,
From the uplands to the sea,
From within and without.
Take care and protect all of the residents
Living in this dwelling.
Shield them from the causes of troubles
That they may encounter.
Here is my humble prayer offering.
It is free of taboo.

HOʻOMAIKAʻI I KA HALE

E ke Akua mana loa,
E nā ʻAumakua mai ka pō mai,
E nā ʻAumakua mai ke ao,
E nā Kiaʻi o kēia wahi,
Eia kā ʻOukou kauwā
ʻO ________________(inoa).
Ke noi aku nei au iā ʻOukou
E nānā mai ʻOukou i kēia hale
Mai luna ā lalo,
Mai kahi kihi ā kahi kihi aʼe,
Mai ka hikina ā ke komohana,
Mai ka uka ā ke kai,
Mai loko ā waho.
E mālama mai a e hoʻomalu iho i ka nohona
  āpau ma kēia wahi.
E pale aku ʻOukou mai nā hoʻopilikia
  ʻana iā lākou.
Eia kaʻu haipule, e hāʻawi ʻia me ka haʻahaʻa.
ʻĀmama. Ua noa.

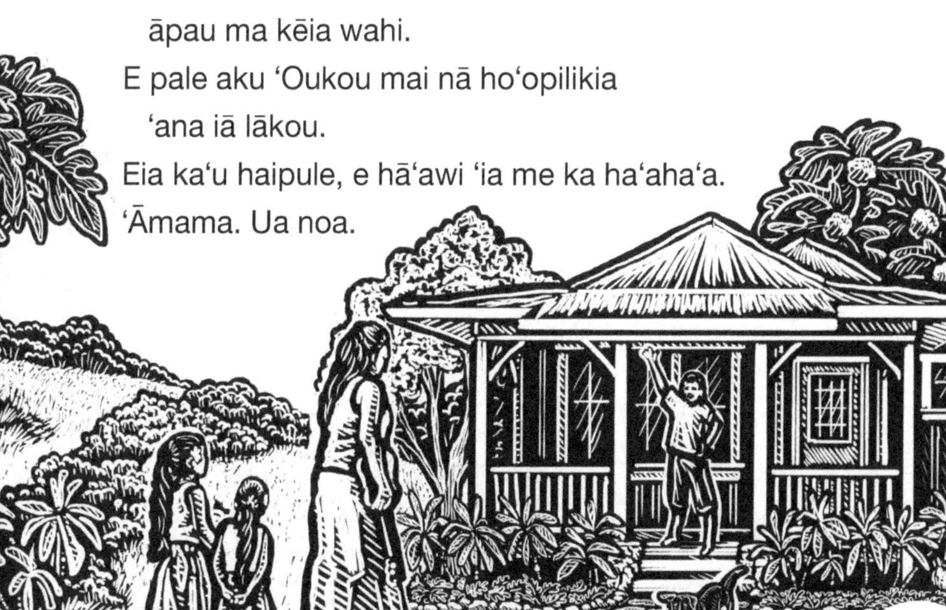

PULE NO KA HEIHEI WA'A – Canoe Racing Prayer

'A'ohe 'auwa'a pa'a i ka hālau i ka mālie.
No canoes remain in the sheds in calm weather.

Pukui, Mary Kawena. 'Ōlelo No'eau. # 129.

KA WA'A – The Canoe

The ancient Hawaiians were a courageous, adventurous, seafaring people. They enjoyed sailing, fishing and had a special passion for the sport of canoe racing. Traditionally, crews in **wa'a kioloa** (racing canoes) would paddle far out to sea and return to the shore. The first canoe to return to the beach was considered the victor. Adapted from an ancient Hawaiian canoe prayer, this **pule** (prayer) seeks special blessings and protection for the canoe and racing crew. It was first performed by Kahu during the Waikiki Yacht Club racing canoe fleet dedication ceremonies which were held on March 12, 2007.

CANOE RACING PRAYER

O Almighty Akua,
The Source of the universe,
We seek and ask
Your blessings.
Take care of this racing canoe and crew.
Guard, guide, instruct, and
Grant success, until the canoe
Lands safely on the seashore.
Here is a prayer offering
Given in the spirit of love and peace.
The prayer is said. All is free of taboo.

PULE NO KA HEIHEI WAʻA

E ke Akua mana loa,
Ke Kumu o ke ao holoʻokoʻa,
Ke ʻimi a noi aku nei mākou
I Kou pōmaikaʻi.
E mālama i kēia waʻa kioloa a me nā mea hoe.
E kiaʻi, e alakaʻi, e hoʻonaʻauao,
E hoʻolanakila, ā pae ʻia ka waʻa
Ma ke ʻaekai me ka mālie.
Eia ka haipule,
I hāʻawi ʻia me ke aloha
A me ka maluhia.
ʻĀmama. Ua noa.

PULE NO KA HOLO'ANA MA KA MOKULELE – Air Travel Prayer

Ke 'imi a noi aku nei mākou i kou pōmaika'i no kā mākou holo'ana ma ka mokulele.
We seek and ask blessings for our air travel journey.

KA HOLO'ANA MA KA MOKULELE – Air Travel

Traditionally, before Hawaiians embarked on a journey, they took time to offer a prayer to ensure a successful voyage and their safe return. This **pule** (prayer) was composed specifically for air travel. It was first performed by Kahu at the blessing of the official inaugural flight of Jet Star Airlines from Hawai'i to Melbourne Australia on December 27th, 2006.

AIR TRAVEL PRAYER

O Almighty Akua,
The One who reigns over heavens and the earth,
I seek and ask now
Your blessing of our journey.
Guide the pilot of this aircraft,
Make ready our flight pathway,
Send forth the favorable winds,
Clear the skies during the day,
Illuminate the stars at night.
Be watchful and take care of us
From the Islands of Hawai'i
Until we arrive in the land of ________________(destination).
Here is my prayer offering
Given in humility and with genuine aloha.
Our prayer has taken flight to protect us
Until our safe return.
The taboo is lifted. All is free.

PULE NO KA HOLOʻANA MA KA MOKULELE

E Ke Akua Mana Loa,
Ke Kumu o ka lani a me ka honua,
Ke ʻimi a noi aku nei au
I Kou pōmaikaʻi no kā mākou holoʻana.
E alakaʻi i ka pailaka o ia mokulele,
E hoʻomākaukau i ke ala hele,
E hoʻouna mai i nā makani ʻoluʻolu,
E hoʻalaneo i ka lewa lani ma ke ao,
E hoʻomālamalama i nā hōkū o ka pō.
E kiaʻi iā mākou
A e mālama pono iā mākou
Mai nā mokupuni o Hawaiʻi
Ā hiki i ka ʻāina o ________________(kahi).
Eia ka haipule, hāʻawi ʻia me ka haʻahaʻa a me ke aloha maoli.
Lele wale aku la ā ka hoʻi ʻana.
ʻĀmama. Ua Noa.

PULE HĀNAI Ā HUHU – Pet Blessing

He ʻīlio welu moe poli.
A well fed dog, sleeps in the bosom.

Pukui, Mary Kawena. ʻŌlelo Noʻeau. # 629.

HĀNAI Ā HUHU – Raising a Pet

The early Hawaiians traditionally domesticated and raised animals as their pets. The custom of pet adoption is called in Hawaiian, **hānai ā huhu**. Customarily, upon acquiring the pet, the **ʻohana** (family) would first choose a befitting name for the animal and welcome it as an extended family member. This **pule** (prayer) asks special blessings for our beloved adopted friends of the animal kingdom. It was composed by Kahu Silva for their family's **hānai ʻīlio** (pet Pomeranians) named Conan and Malia.

PET BLESSING PRAYER

O Ke Akua, the Source of all creation,
The earth is full of your glory.
You have given mankind
Dominion over all the creatures of nature.
I extend heartfelt gratitude
And praise to You.
I beseech now Your blessings.
Here is my beloved pet,
_________________________(name),
My adopted companion, a friend to go with,
A friend to sleep and play with.
Please care for, protect, and
Bless him/her always.
Fill his/her life with happiness
And many good years.
I place now his/her well-being in Your good hands.

—Amen

PULE HĀNAI Ā HUHU

E ke Akua, ke Kumu o nā mea āpau,
Ua piha ka honua i Kou nani.
Nāu i lilo nā kānaka
I kahu o nā holoholona āpau.
Ke hoʻouna aku nei au i ka mahalo
Me ka hoʻomaikaʻi iā ʻOe.
Ke noi aku nei au i Kou pōmaikaʻi.
Eia ka hānai ā huhu, kuʻu mea aloha nani
ʻO____________________(inoa),
Kuʻu hoa hānai, hoa hele,
Hoa moe, a hoa pāʻani.
E ʻoluʻolu ʻOe, e hoʻomālama,
E hoʻomalu, a e hoʻomaikaʻi mau iāia.
E hoʻopiha i kōna ola me ka hauʻoli
A me nā makahiki maikaʻi.
Ke waiho nei au i kōna ola i Kou mau lima maikaʻi.

— *ʻĀmene*

PULE NO KA HELE WĀWAE ʻANA – Walkathon Prayer

Pāpahi i ka hae o ka lanakila.
Honor the flag of the victor.

Pukui, Mary Kawena. ʻŌlelo Noʻeau. # 2600.

KA HELE WĀWAE ʻANA – The Walkathon

The Ancient Hawaiians enjoyed participating in competitive sports, contests, games and non-competitive recreational activities as a traditional part of their daily lifestyle. Free time during the day might be spent **ʻauʻana** (swimming), **pae i ka nalu** (surfing), or **hoʻolele lupe** (kite flying) while evenings were perhaps more conducive to a quiet game of **kōnane** (Hawaiian checkers). Each year during a four-month long makahiki festival they celebrated the harvest with religious rituals and a variety of athletic contests. This prayer was first performed by Kahu as an invocation for the Hawaiʻi Parkinson 3K Charity Walkathon held on Oct. 22, 2016.

WALKATHON PRAYER

To You, Ke Akua,
The Divine Source of all existence,
We dedicate this special day and consecrate this
charity walk event in Your honor.
We beseech You now to bestow Your blessings upon all
of the people here with us in support of this walkathon.
Strengthen them in body, mind, and spirit.
Guide them safely along the designated route to its finish.
We humbly ask these things
in the sacred name of the Holy Spirit.
Here is our fervent prayer offering
Given in the spirit of aloha
And in the name of peace.
The prayer has flown to the heavens.
All is free.

PULE NO KA HELE WĀWAE ʻANA

E Ke Akua,
Ke Kumu o ke ao holoʻokoʻa,
Ke hoʻolaʻa aku nei mākou
I kēia lā a me kēia hele wāwae ʻana iā ʻOe.
Ke noi aku nei mākou
I Kou pōmaikaʻi i nā poʻe āpau
I hui pū me mākou no ke kōkua ʻana
Me kēia hele ʻana.
E hoʻoikaika ʻOe i kō lākou mau kino,
Kō lākou mau manaʻo,
A me kō lākou mau mana.
Ke alakaʻi nei ʻOe
  iā lākou ma ke ala hele.
Ke noi aku nei mākou
I nēia mau mea me ka haʻahaʻa
Ma ka inoa o ka ʻUhane Hemolele.
Eia ka haipule,
I hāʻawi ʻia me ke aloha
A me ka maluhia.
ʻĀmama, Ua noa.

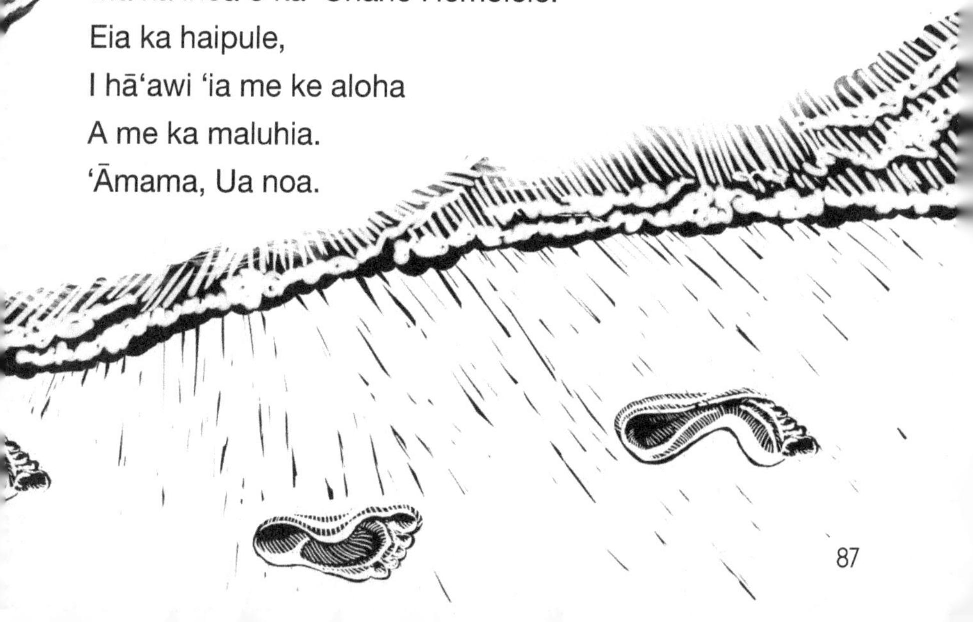

PULE NO KE KĀLAI ʻANA I KA LĀʻAU – Tree Cutting Prayer

He keiki aloha nā mea kanu.
Beloved children are the plants.

Pukui, Mary Kawena. ʻŌlelo Noʻeau. # 684.

KĀLAI ʻANA I KA LĀʻAU – Tree Cutting

The early Hawaiians were traditionally an agrarian society. They believed that every indigenous plant was a gift of the gods. Certain plants were also spiritually revered as the **kino lau** (earthly forms) of the sacred Hawaiian deities. The following prayer is adapted from an ancient Hawaiian tree cutting prayer and includes a provision for a **hoʻokupu** or ritual offering. It is considered approprate for the ceremonial hewing of a tree that may be diseased, unsafe, a danger or an obstruction to the landowner.

TREE CUTTING PRAYER

O heavenly Akua (God),
Look upon Your devoted servant,
________________(name).
Here is the tree (old) (unsafe) (of no value).
Therefore, it is appropriate to hew the trunk of this tree.
We beseech You to permit us to cut down this tree.
Look favorably upon this (axe) (saw).
Do not let it cut crookedly.
Cause the tree to fall in a clear, safe place.
Here is the offering, a compensatory gift freely given
in the spirit of aloha.
We humbly ask these things in our prayer request.
It is within Your power to grant O Ke Akua.
The taboo is lifted. All is free.

PULE NO KE KĀLAI ʻANA I KA LĀʻAU

E kuʻu Akualani,
E huli mai, e nānā i Kāu kauwā,
iā ________________(inoa).
Eia ke kumulāʻau (kahiko) (maluʻole) (waiwaiʻole).
Nolaila, he pono ke kua i ke kumu o kēia
kumulaʻau.
E ʻoluʻolu ʻOe, e ʻae mai nei iā mākou
E ʻoki i kēia kumulāʻau.
E nānā pono mai ʻOe i kēia (koʻi) (pahi olo).
Aʻole ʻOe e hoʻopā kua.
E hoʻohina aʻe ʻOe ma kahi mālaʻelaʻe.
Eia ka ʻālana, he uku, he makana
Hāʻawi ʻia me ke aloha.
Ke noi aku nei mākou i kēia mau mea
me ka haʻahaʻa.
ʻO Kāu ia, e ke Akua, e hāʻawi ai.
ʻĀmama. Ua noa.

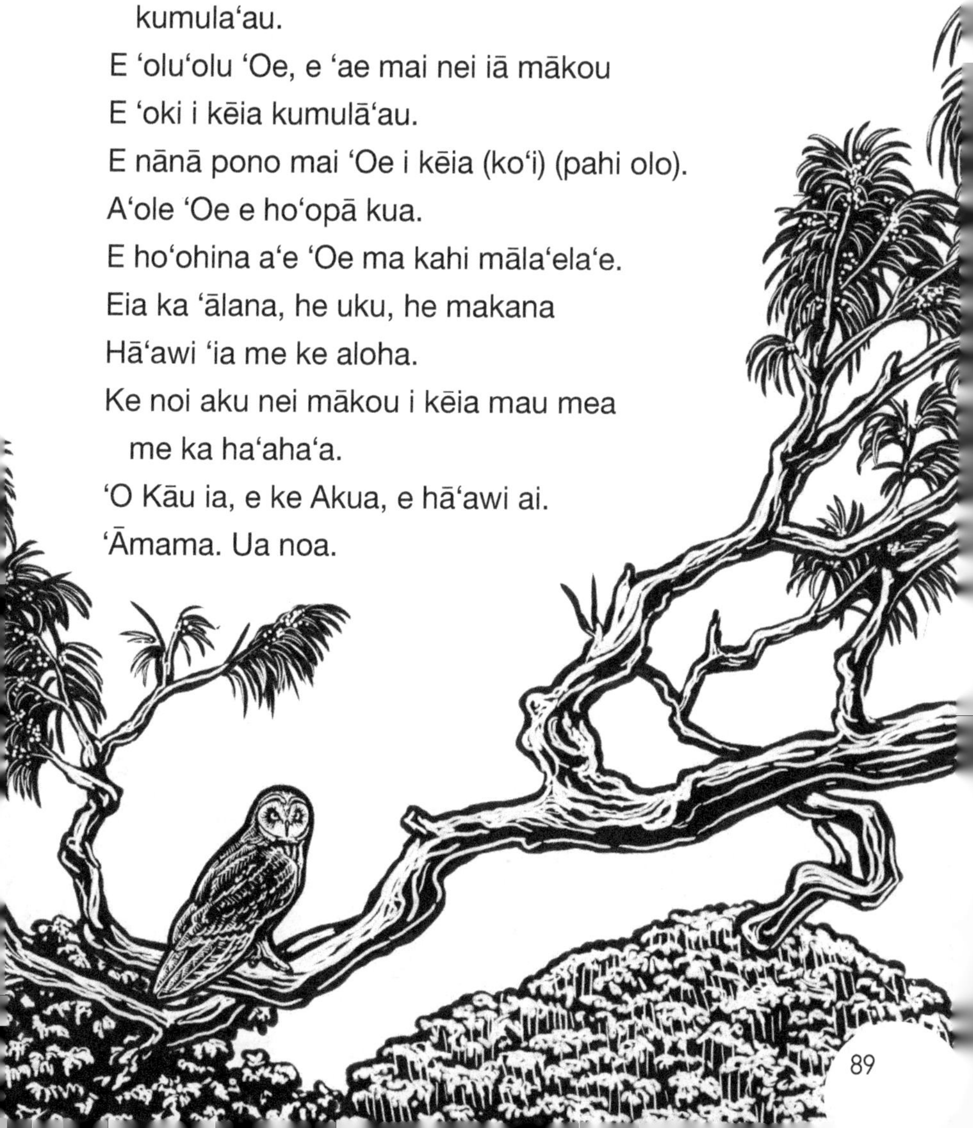

PULE PANINA – Closing Prayer

E lawe i ke a'o a mālama, a e 'oi mau ka na'auao.
He who takes his teachings and applies them increases his knowledge.

Pukui, Mary Kawena. 'Ōlelo No'eau. # 328.

PANINA – Closing

The ancient Hawaiians beheld the dual nature of all things. They believed that every life event had a beginning and an ending. Whenever they gathered for a purpose, they traditionally began the occasion with an opening prayer called a **Pule Wehena** to unite everyone and concluded with a closing prayer or **Pule Panina**. This prayer expresses gratitude to those who have come from near and far to share their aloha and asks for their safe return to their home and the warm embrace of their loved ones.

CLOSING PRAYER

O Heavenly God,
The Source of all knowledge
Great and small,
We have gathered together at this assembly
for the purpose of sharing our helpful insights
and discussing relevant issues with one another.
We have fulfilled our responsibilities
And we have successfully completed our work.
We ask now Your blessings
On the people who have come
From near and far
And united with us in the spirit of aloha.
Guide them now safely on the journey
To their homes and return them to
The welcoming embrace of their loved ones.
Here is our fervent closing prayer
Given with humility.
It is finished. All is free.

PULE PANINA

E Ke Akua Lani,
Ke Kumu o ka ʻike nui
A me ka ʻike iki,
Ua hoʻākoakoa ʻia mākou ma kēia ʻaha kūkākūkā
no ka haʻawina i kō mākou manaʻo akamai
a me ke kamaʻilio ʻana o nā kumuhana a kekahi
me kekahi.
Ua hoʻopau ʻia kō mākou mau kuleana a ua
pono kā mākou mau hana.
Ke noi aku nei mākou
I Kou pōmaikaʻi i ka poʻe i hele mai ō a ʻaneʻi
a hui pū ʻia me mākou me ka ʻuhane o ke aloha.
E ʻalakaʻi aku iā lākou ma ke ala i kō lākou mau
hale a e hoʻi hou iā lākou i ka poʻe e aloha nui
ai me ka maluhia.
Eia kā mākou pule kāhea
E hāʻawi ʻia aku nei me ka haʻahaʻa.
ʻĀmama. Ua noa.

ʻŌLELO PĀKUʻI
Appendix

KA PALAPALA NOI NO NĀ PULE –
Prayer Request Form

The Ke Aloha O Kalani Ministry is dedicated to preserving, perpetuating and promoting the sacred beliefs and ancient spiritual wisdom of our Native Hawaiian ancestors. As a believer in the power of prayer, Kahu Silva would be pleased to pray for you and your special intentions. Please email us at either **aokpray@gmail.com, alohaokalaniministry@gmail.com** or complete this form to let us know how Kahu can help you or a special person in your life.

Ke Aloha O Kalani Ministry
c/o Hawaii Cultural Services, LLC
PO Box 4782
Kāneʻohe, Hawaiʻi 96744

Name ________________________________ Date ____________

Address ____

City ___________________________ State_______ Zip _________

Email____

Prayer Request (please print legibly)

____

____

____

____

____

( ) Confidential

THOUGHTS AND REFLECTIONS

THOUGHTS AND REFLECTIONS

PAPA KUHIKUHI O NĀ PUKE I HELUHELU ‘IA
Bibliography

Beckwith, Martha, *Hawaiian Mythology.* Honolulu: University Press of Hawai‘i 1970.

Beckwith, Martha, (translator, editor, and commentator), *The Kumulipo: A Hawaiian Creation Chant.* Chicago: The University of Chicago Press, 1951.

Cunningham, Scott, *Hawaiian Magic & Spirituality.* St. Paul, Minnesota: Lewellyn Publications, 2000.

Dudley, Michael Kioni, *Man, Gods and Nature: A Hawaiian Nation I.* Honolulu: Nā Kāne O ka Malo Press, 1990.

Good News Bible with Deuterocanonicals/Apocrypha, Today's English Version, American Bible Society, New York *Imprimatur:* John Frances Whealon Archbishop of Hartford, *Censor deputatus:* The Reverend Kenneth H. Shiner May 15, 1978.

Gutmanis, June, *Nā Pule Kahiko: Ancient Hawaiian Prayers.* Honolulu: Editions Limited, 1983.

Handy, E. S. Craighill and Mary Kawena Pukui, *The Polynesian Family System in Ka-ū.* Hawai‘i. 1958. Reprinted Rutland (Vermont): Charles E. Tuttle, 1972.

Judd, Henry P., *The Hawaiian Language.* Honolulu Hawaiian Service, Inc.1939.

Kalakaua, King David, *The Legends and Myths of Hawai‘i,* 1888. Reprinted Rutland (Vermont): Charles E Tuttle, 1972.

Kamakau, Samuel Manaiakalani, *Ka Po‘e Kahiko: The People of Old,* Mary Kawena Pukui, translator. Honolulu: Bishop Museum Press, 1964.

Kamakau, Samuel Manaiakalani, *Nā Hana a ka Po‘e Kahiko: The Works of the People of Old.* Mary Kawena Pukui, translator. Honolulu: Bishop Museum Press, 1976.

Kent, Harold Winfield, *Treasury of Hawaiian Words in One Hundred and One Categories.* Masonic Public Library of Hawai'i, 1986.

Malo, David, *Mo'olelo Hawai'i (Hawaiian Antiquities).* Nathaniel B. Emerson, translator. 1898. Reprinted Honolulu: Bishop Museum Press, 1971.

McBride, L. R., *The Kahuna: Versatile Mystics of Old Hawai'i.* Hilo (Hawai'i): Petroglyph Press, 1972.

Pukui, Mary Kawena and Samuel H. Elbert, *Hawaiian Dictionary.* Honolulu: University of Hawai'i Press, 1986.

Pukui, Mary Kawena, *'Ōlelo No'eau: Hawaiian Proverbs and Poetical Saying.* Honolulu: Bishop Museum Press, 1983.

Pukui, Mary Kawena, E. W. Haertig, and Catherine A Lee, *Nānā I Ke Kumu (Look to the Source), Volume I.* Honolulu: Hui Hānai, Queen Lili'uokalani Children's Center, 1972.

Pukui, Mary Kawena, E. W. Haertig, and Catherine A Lee, *Nānā I Ke Kumu (Look to the Source), Volume II.* Honolulu: Hui Hānai, Queen Lili'uokalani Children's Center, 1972.

Pukui, Mary Kawena, Samuel H. Elbert, and Esther T. Mookini, *Place Names of Hawai'i.* Honolulu: The University Press of Hawai'i, 1974.

Yardley, Laura Kealoha, *The Heart of Huna.* Honolulu: Advanced Neuro Dynamics 1990.

Silva, Agnes B. Personal Interviews 1968 - 2013.

Craver, Malia Personal Interviews 1983 - 1989.

HAWAI'I CULTURAL SERVICES (HCS)

HCS is a State of Hawai'i LLC organization whose services and management are based on traditional Hawaiian **kahuna** (shamanistic) expertise, teachings, values and native holistic healing practices. Foremost among the many Hawaiian values that HCS embraces and advocates is the core guiding principle of PONO, the Hawaiian word for doing what is morally, ethically, culturally, traditionally and spiritually right for the well-being of our indigenous people. HCS offers an array of cultural and educational services including workshops, lectures, seminars, programs and activities designed to preserve, promote and perpetuate the sacred beliefs and ancient wisdom of our revered Native Hawaiian ancestors. Our primary mission is to communicate, share and disseminate a legacy of traditional knowledge unique to our proud Native Hawaiian heritage. We accomplish this through the creation of traditional learning opportunities as well as the production, publication and distribution of educational information, materials and resources. In addition, we fulfill our goals by engaging with other organizations nationally and internationally through the facilitation of exchange programs and global networking, via our website under the domain name **www.KahunaTeachings.com**. We are dedicated to improving the overall quality of life and furthering the overall spiritual well-being of all indigenous peoples.

Made in USA - Kendallville, IN
1162343_9780986012235
09.10.2020 0839